In this treasury of devotional thoughts, Alison Daunton-Fear inspires the readers to live a kingdom-min~~ded~~ ~~and Ch~~ ~~i~~ ~~esire to~~ encourage people to grow in int ~~ad a life~~ totally dependent on God and se  ~~eir daily~~ life, shines through the pages of ~~wisdom~~ Alison brings in here are biblical ~~ese also~~ seem to echo the cry of a heart th ~~rvice of~~ Christ and sincere love for others.

Rev. Dr. V. J. Samkutty

Academic Vice-Principal, All Nations Christian College, Ware

Alison Daunton-Fear was a devout Christian and a staunch member of the Mothers' Union. Her writings offer wisdom and understanding of the teaching of the Bible. In her talk 'Treasure in Heaven' she speaks of keeping treasures and clinging to them saying, 'I wouldn't lose them for the world.' These writings are Alison's treasure and can now be shared with us. Although they are writings for her time and Mothers' Union has moved on, our organization still holds Alison's implicit belief that prayer and the nurture of children and family life are vital to society. Enjoy reading them, and possibly using them in your own talks.

Nikki Sweatman

Mothers' Union Provincial President & Worldwide Trustee, Canterbury Province

The virtuous woman of Proverbs 31, it seems, has put pen to paper. The fruit of her hands makes rewarding reading. She is economical with words but generous with her knowledge. In every circumstance and opportunity she brings comfort and encouragement. She is wise and winsome but above all compassionate. She fears no man but only her Lord. Alison's children honour her with this collection so that we also might surrender to Jesus and be free.

Michael Collie

National Director, SparkLit
(Society for Promoting Christian Knowledge, Australia)

I met my friend Andrew's mother in Worthing in 1997. It was a pleasure to talk with the kind and wise old lady. Later, reading her talks I enjoyed the clear and poetic language and I was moved by the contents of these texts. From John's First Epistle we know: God is love. I think Alison Daunton-Fear's thoughts are interpretations of these words. Even the talks given during the war are full of love for the suffering people. There is no hatred of the enemies. What a genuine Christian tone! The readers of this book will become infected by this spirit.

Helmut Wilhelm

Prädikant, Evangelishe Kirchengemeinde Lichtenberg, Berlin.

Alison Daunton-Fear during the war.

Treasures from a Deep Mine

Readings for Lent and Daily Life

Alison Daunton-Fear

edited and introduced by
Andrew Daunton-Fear and Mary Treacher

O&U
Onwards & Upwards

Onwards and Upwards Publishers

4 The Old Smithy

London Road

Rockbeare,

EX5 2EA

United Kingdom.

www.onwardsandupwards.org

First edition, published in the United Kingdom by Onwards and Upwards Publishers (2020).

ISBN:	978-1-78815-517-5
Typeface:	Sabon LT

In loving memory

of

Dora Helen Robertson

(1876-1965)

Foreword

Several of these reflections refer to the significance of women in history and not least in the story of Christian witness. Surely Alison Daunton-Fear must be included in that list. Like countless other women she showed a remarkable capacity for touching many hearts while fulfilling a demanding partnership with a busy husband and bringing up her children.

These gems of Christian insight light up biblical truth in a simple and accessible way and with a freshness which comes from the immediate contexts in which they were offered. Part of the charm which Alison displays derives from her worldwide experience in India, Australia and England. Each of the contributions come from a particular stage in the crises which befell the first part of twentieth century.

That immediate context stimulates thoughts from where we are in the family of God with our struggling faith, our longing for peace and our intentions to be lights in our generation.

We can only imagine what a powerful impact some of Alison's phrases had on her listeners – "what sleep and rest are to restoring the body, so prayer is in restoring the soul" ... "the legacy of Jesus is peace" ... "the treasure we bring to God" ... "the looks between his eyes and ours" ... a meditation on "hands".

We owe a debt to Mary, Andrew and Ruth for resurrecting and editing these talks so that the wisdom of their mother can inspire a generation which she never knew.

Michael Turnbull
Bishop of Durham, 1994-2003
Bishop of Rochester, 1988-1994

Contents

Acknowledgements

We would like first to acknowledge our indebtedness to our sister Ruth Sinker, who has been our partner throughout the preparation of this book, and to her husband Nigel for helpful advice. Then, we wish to express our great gratitude to the Rt. Revd. Michael Turnbull, Andrew's diocesan bishop when he took up ministry in the parish of Barming, Kent in 1989, for his most kind and careful Foreword. We deeply appreciate too the tributes to Mother by Joy Lancaster and Daphne Wilson in Australia, with whom we have been in correspondence, and are glad to add to them those of Fran Newling and the Rev. John Clarke. We are particularly grateful also for the warm commendations of Mother's talks given by the Rev. Dr. V. J. Samkutty, Academic Vice-Principal of All Nations Christian College, Ware; by Nikki Sweatman, Mothers' Union Provincial President and Worldwide Trustee, Canterbury Province; by Michael Collie, National Director of SparkLit (Society for Promoting Christian Knowledge, Australia); and by our friend Helmut Wilhelm in Berlin. Helmut's church, Evangelische Kirchengemeinde, Lichtenberg, entered into a much-valued partnership with St. Margaret's Barming in 1996 which has continued to this day.

We are grateful also to our cousin Catherine Van den Bosch (née Turnbull) and her sister-in-law Susan Turnbull for information about the Robertson family; to Sister Frances Dominica of All Saints' Convent, Oxford, for putting us in touch with Claire Childs, archivist, who most kindly searched until she found information on our aunt Winifred Robertson's connection with the Society of All Saints Sisters of the Poor; to Frances Walker, librarian of All Nations Christian College, Ware, for kindly facilitating research in the archives of Ridgelands Bible College; to archivist Catherine Wakeling for kindly pinpointing documents in the USPG archives held in the Bodleian Library, Oxford, that might give information about the Rev. G. R. ('Nobby') Clarke; and to the staff of the South West Heritage Trust centre in Taunton for making available archive material of the parish of Street. Thanks are also due to Pavlos Triantaris and Rosemary Pope for kindly finding out the authorship of a poem and a hymn respectively quoted by Mother; and to Shelby Boland, Personal Assistant of the present Principal of Westcott House, Cambridge for information about Father's time at Westcott. We also express our appreciation to Kath Barnett for her valuable suggestions on the layout of the text of Mother's talks, and to the Rev. Jean Thorn for her prayerful advice about publication and the potential use of the talks as an aid to meditation. Mary Whettem and Rose Sangster have given us their unwavering interest and encouragement throughout the project as have the members of the Beaminster Prayers for Healing Group. For several months individual talks were shared with this group in the context of worship. They helped to focus our minds on the greatness of God's love and mercy and his unfailing concern for each of his children. We are also indebted to Karel (Charles) Herman for technical advice.

Nearly half of Mother's talks printed in this book were delivered in Australia so, in addition to those who composed tributes, we would like to thank Miriam Newall, Diocesan Secretary of the Diocese of Armidale, and Colin Reilly, editor of The Anglican Church of Australia Directory, for information about Curates of St. John's Tamworth during our parents' time in Tamworth; also Shirley Dawson for kindly searching at the Armidale Archive Centre for records of Mother's talks given in Armidale Diocese away from Tamworth; also the Rev. Dr. Charles Sherlock and Tory Greeney for their help and encouragement generally.

Finally, we would like to thank the Rev. John Huggett for suggesting we approach Onwards and Upwards to publish this book. We did, and have found Luke Jeffery and his team there of the utmost help at each stage of the publication process, for which we are deeply grateful.

Editorial Comments

Early in 2018 we came across a script of one of our mother's devotional talks in her own handwriting. We quickly named it 'The Dew'. We were impressed by its originality of thought and its spirituality. We shared it with several other people who were likewise impressed. Then a search was made of family papers and, to our surprise, there were well over a hundred other scripts of talks given by Mother over the course of half a century. Many we found very moving. One of us typed these out, and shared some with others, again generally receiving an enthusiastic response. From them we and our sister Ruth have selected the forty which are in this present volume.

Some of these talks were written out in full, others were partly in note form. All had numbered sections. We have taken out most of the numbering to facilitate easier reading, and where they were in note form, we have 'joined the dots', believing we know our mother's mind pretty well. Where, however, she has used just one or two words to refer to an illustration she told her audience direct, we have usually had to admit defeat and leave these out, unless we have been very familiar with the story concerned.

We have placed the talks within a chronological framework of five periods: Early Ministry, War and Peace, Gravesend and Hove, Tamworth N.S.W., and Adelaide, prefaced by a biographical Introduction. Relatively few of the scripts record the date and place of the talk's delivery. Where they do, we have recorded these in a footnote. For the rest, we have been guided by two factors: handwriting and internal evidence. It so happens our mother's handwriting somewhat changed after the war. The scripts of her earlier talks are written in smaller, rather neater letters, usually in blue-black ink. From Gravesend onwards, for the rest of her life, her lettering tended to be larger, rounder and usually written in royal blue ink. Internal evidence includes references to current wartime, indicating the talk was given in Street, and allusions to the Tamworth hills, the 'Festival of Light' or the lateness of the hour, indicating they were delivered in Tamworth, the last-mentioned as radio epilogues (all written out in full). In some cases we cannot be certain where the talk was delivered; such talks we have allocated to a period in which they *might well* have been given.

To some of her talks Mother gave titles. These we have retained. To the rest we have ourselves given titles, based on the talks' contents, for ease of identification. For her talks Mother invariably used her beloved Scofield Reference Authorised (King James) Version of the Bible. She came to know its contents very well, using it always in her daily Quiet Time. Father readily admitted that she knew the Bible better than he did! But today many readers are put off by the archaic word forms of the Authorised Version. So, where these occur, we have substituted the wording of the New King James Version.

When Mother's scripts contain Bible references, in some cases we have transferred these to footnotes, to facilitate smoother reading. When she quotes or alludes to Bible verses without giving references, for the convenience of readers we have supplied the appropriate references in footnotes. When quoting from memory or, adapting the text to bring its meaning across more forcefully to her audience, Mother has not quoted a passage exactly, we have prefaced the reference in the footnote with 'cf.' ('compare'). When quoting from sources other than Scripture, Mother usually acknowledges whom she is quoting, but she rarely mentions the writing concerned; in delivering a devotional talk this would have been an interruption. But we, as editors, have tried to trace the source of these quotations, and acknowledge them in footnotes. When we have failed to find them, we have at least tried to give a little information about the writer/speaker concerned. Occasionally we have felt the need to correct in a footnote something Mother has said in the text. In such cases she may have been following what was commonly believed at the time she spoke but is now not accepted. If the ending of some of her talks seems abrupt, probably it is because she closed with a prayer which she has not recorded. Indeed, she may have closed most, if not all, of her talks with a prayer.

We commend them all now to you for private reading and reflection, perhaps in Lent, though by no means only then. Some may be found valuable for use by study groups and at retreats or quiet days. Many we believe will speak to men as well as women.

A.D-F.
M.W.T.

Introduction

Alison Dora Isabella was born on October 11, 1911, the youngest child of Andrew and Dora Robertson. Her father had been born in 1860 into a farming family in Kinghorn, Fife, but when he was only six, his mother died, and he was brought up by an aunt in Edinburgh. In 1882 he went overseas to work in the National Bank of India. In India he met the beautiful Dora Stranack, of part-Irish extraction, but born in Bombay in 1876. They married and their first three children were born in India: Derrick, Kenneth and Winifred. In 1906, after 24 years in India, the last ten years as manager of the Madras branch of the National Bank of India, ill-health forced Andrew to retire. A valedictory scroll given him by his bank staff in Madras was warm in its appreciation of all that he had done for them. He then took his family to live in Hove in Sussex. There Alison was born. When World War I broke out he moved the family to Boscombe, west Hampshire, believing that, as it was further from London, it would be safer. Derrick and Kenneth went into the army, but Derrick was killed at Neuve Chapelle in 1915 and Kenneth was invalided out with a severely damaged knee. Their father was distraught at Derrick's death and railed against God, declaring he was an atheist. He was a man of strong emotions which sometimes he was able to express in the poetry he wrote. At other times he just fell into black moods, which now would probably be described as depression. During these, no-one dared approach him except his little daughter, whom he dearly loved. Sadly, he died in 1924 when she was only twelve.

Dora was a devout Anglo-Catholic and imparted her faith to her three remaining children. Winifred, deeply shocked by her father's atheism, and wishing to atone for him, joined the Society of All Saints Sisters of the Poor as a novice in 1926, but had to withdraw after a few months to look after her sick mother. She continued an ordered life of prayer and, in 1928, joined the Community of the Healing Saviour, where she was known as 'Sister Anastasia'. Some years later she went with her mother to assist Fr. John Maillard at Milton Abbey in Dorset, a centre of divine healing. Kenneth meanwhile had returned to India to work in the Mercantile Bank. He travelled about a fair bit and, in Ceylon, met and married Aileen whose family owned a tea plantation. After Alison had finished her schooling, her mother took her out to India to stay with Kenneth and Aileen. She loved the social life under the white Raj and particularly dancing. But she also became aware of some of the deep needs of Indian society and, it seems, began to wonder about future missionary work there.

After they returned to England, Dora and Alison went to Bude in Cornwall for their summer holidays. At that time, a lively CSSM[1] children's mission was held there each August. The team of young leaders would have built a sand pulpit on the beach from which they presented the gospel to the many children on holiday through Bible stories, choruses and in various entertaining ways. The team leader in 1928 was the Rev. Hugh Gough, later Bishop of Barking in east London, and subsequently Archbishop of Sydney. It would seem Alison's love of children led her to get involved as a helper. Entries in one of her notebooks show she attended also in 1929 and 1930. It appears that the gospel message presented to the children deeply touched her own heart. Ever afterwards she spoke of having been spiritually 'quickened' then. Others might call this conversion; certainly, it changed her whole outlook. Each of these years the lady leader of the mission was Miss D. M. Burton, Vice Principal of Ridgelands Bible College. She must have taken a favourable report to the Principal, Mrs. Howard Hooker, for an invitation was then sent to Alison to come and study at the College, which prepared women for Christian service at home and abroad. Alison was interested until she received the course syllabus in which, she said, she was horrified to see all the 'ologies' to be studied! She felt herself no scholar but, praying about it and reading her Bible, she was challenged by the verse, "No man, having put his hand to the plough, and looking back, is fit for the kingdom of God."[2] She enrolled, it appears, in the autumn of 1931, and thereafter threw herself heart and soul into the life of the College. The previous Christmas her mother had given her as a present a Scofield Reference Bible, which became her constant companion at the College, and indeed for the rest of her life.

Ridgelands was an interdenominational Bible College, founded by Mr. and Mrs. Howard Hooker in 1919. Mrs. Hooker had, through her involvement with the Zenana Bible and Medical Mission, become aware there was a great need for Bible teaching and character training for young women desiring to take up mission work. After much prayer and sharing her vision with others, she and her husband, a lawyer, raised £10,000 for the purchase of a large private mansion, set in 3½ acres of ground, on the Ridgeway across Wimbledon Common in London. A two-year diploma course was offered. The syllabus enabled the whole Bible to be studied in two years. Each book was analysed individually, and additional attention was given to learning the great stories of the Bible. The students were expected to memorise some passages of Scripture, and matters of biblical criticism were not ignored. Mrs Hooker, it seems, undertook much of the Bible teaching herself, for she had previously attended Bible classes of the renowned expositor Dr. G. Campbell Morgan, and had then lectured at a Bible College on Clapham Common whose principal was the Rev. Oswald Chambers. Besides attending two hours of morning lectures, students at Ridgelands were expected to devote two further hours to private Bible study in the afternoons. Sometimes there were evening lectures by visiting speakers. Other subjects in the course included church history, the Prayer Book, personal evangelism, missionary principles and methods, the comparative study of religions, Sunday School methods, child study and the psychology of teaching, and speech training. There was a daily framework of public worship and private prayer. The students slept three to five in dormitories, their beds separated by curtains. They were entirely responsible for the cleaning of the college. They also had a hand in their own government, a team of three students being elected each term to provide leadership and organisation. Each of the three served as Senior Student for three weeks and then relinquished the post, to teach them how to take up authority, and how to serve under others. The students also gained plenty of practical experience from going out in teams some afternoons and evenings to Fulham for a whole range of activities with youth and women and for house-to-house visiting. They led a dinner-hour service at Summerstown laundry, and were involved with Bermondsey Medical Mission and Chelsea Rescue Home. On Sundays they took Sunday Schools and Bible Classes.[3]

The students were also allowed time for recreation. Alison showed a talent for acting, once playing Shylock in Shakespeare's *Merchant of Venice*, wearing a false nose! Alas, one time when she was Senior Student, she had her hair cut and permed, and was reprimanded by her Principal with the words, "A woman's hair is her glory!" Though records have not been preserved, Alison must have graduated in the summer of 1933. Her great desire upon leaving the College was to go out to southern India to join the noted missionary Amy Carmichael in her work of rescuing children from child prostitution in Hindu temples. But it so happened that, as part of her training, she attended the ordination as priest of the handsome young Curate of St. John's Deptford, Richard (Dick) Daunton Fear in his parish church by the Bishop of Southwark,[4] on December 27, 1932.[5] She said later that she 'noticed' him then, and subsequently they were introduced by a mutual friend, Wendy Clark. Dick Fear had been involved in CSSM missions in his home town of Burnham-on-Sea in Somerset and, after graduating from Cambridge University, had trained for the Church of England ministry at the London College of Divinity, where he became Senior Student. The couple fell deeply in love and on April 9, 1934 they married. Henceforth Alison's missionary work was to take the form of assisting her husband in his ministry.

Their first parish was Woolland in Dorset, followed in 1935 by Aspenden in Hertfordshire, where Mary, their first daughter, was born. The next year they moved on to the united benefice of Denton with South Heighton and Tarring Neville in east Sussex which gave them valuable rural pastoral experience. Richard was appointed Vicar of Lindfield in 1938, but two years later, in an exchange of livings, he returned to his home county of Somerset to become Rector of Street. There he was near his family in Burnham and able to visit his father who was seriously ill. It was wartime and, though no bombs fell on Street, children from London were evacuated there to foster homes, and army regiments camped in Nissen huts on the cricket field. From January 1940 there was food rationing and, from June 1941, clothes rationing, which put an end to the lucrative annual church sales of work.[6] In addition, daily radio broadcasts kept the residents of the town abreast of all the developments in the war. Minutes of the Parochial Church Council show Alison was appointed a member of that Council in June 1940; and at the Annual Parochial Church Meeting in April 1941 she was chosen to be one of the PCC's representatives on the Ruri-Decanal Conference, equivalent today to the Deanery Synod. In the Minutes of the APCM in 1942 it is noted that she had consented to become "enroller", i.e. leader of the parish's Mothers' Union. She clearly felt in full sympathy with Mary Sumner, the movement's founder, in her emphasis on prayer and her desire that mothers should use their unique opportunity to foster in their children habits of prayer and Bible reading. Scripts of a number of Alison's talks from those war years have survived; most appear to have been addressed to the Street Mothers' Union branch, but their contents surely deserve a far wider audience. How finely they encouraged faith at that time of crisis! A further address may have been given at a Ruri-Decanal Conference.[7] In 1944 the family moved to Malvern in Worcestershire, where Richard became Vicar of Holy Trinity Church and Chaplain of Malvern Girls' College. There he established his name as a preacher. During that time their son Andrew was born. But Richard really wanted a big challenge, and that was certainly granted when in 1948 he was appointed Rector, and subsequently Rural Dean, of Gravesend in Kent.

Gravesend was a tough parish with four churches: St. George's, St. James', St. Mary's, and Holy Trinity with St. Andrew's waterside chapel. These were of varying churchmanship, and each had its own PCC and expected a full array of services. The Rector had to provide these with the assistance of two or three Curates and the help of retired clergy. At the end of World War II all the churches were dilapidated, and the Diocese of Rochester put forward a series of reorganisation schemes to simplify the situation. The Bishop, it seems, favoured one that entailed the demolition of St. George's Church. But this was the only historic church of the town (built in 1731), and under its chancel lay the remains of American heroine Pocahontas.[8] Many protested, both in England and America. Then, Sir Evelyn Wrench, founder of the English-Speaking Union, wrote a letter in *The Times* suggesting St. George's should be made an ecumenical Chapel of Unity. The idea found support, and the Rector, assisted by his voluntary secretary, Miss Joan Apperley, took up the challenge of raising the money for its restoration. Appeal letters were sent far and wide, and in America it was agreed that, if half the money required was raised in England, they would contribute the rest. In October 1951 Richard, with Alison and Joan Apperley, set out on a 17,000-mile preaching tour of the eastern states of North America.[9] All the money needed[10] was raised within one year, and on November 1, 1952 St. George's was dedicated by the Bishop of Rochester, the Rt. Revd. Christopher Chavasse, as the first ecumenical Chapel of Unity in England. The preacher was the Rev. Dr. William Edwin Sangster, former President of the Methodist Conference, and American-born Viscountess Nancy Astor, first female member of the British Parliament, played a part in the service.[11] With the change in status of St. George's, St. James' became the parish church of Gravesend, and Holy Trinity and St. Andrew's became chapels of ease. In May 1951 St. Mary's had been given a parish of its own.

Alison played an important part in church life, despite the demands of family life, particularly with the birth of her third child, Ruth, in February 1949. Gravesend had an established Mothers' Union branch, which she may have led. There was also a Young Wives' Fellowship, which met one evening a month at the Rectory. In May 1951 another women's group was started called 'The Martha and Mary Meeting'. Alison was its leader. Such a group was particularly close to her heart as it combined the domestic and spiritual aspects of a Christian mother's life. As both the Mothers' Union and Young Wives' Fellowship met in the first week of the month, this new group quickly settled into meeting one afternoon in each of the other weeks. While Alison gave some of the talks, there were also visiting speakers. But the strain of his very demanding ministry in Gravesend took its toll of her husband, and he resigned early in 1953.[12]

After some months, the Rt. Revd. George Bell, Bishop of Chichester, offered Richard the parish of St. Philip's Hove on the Sussex coast. Here he could recover, and it was hoped that his son Andrew, who had become asthmatic in Gravesend, might benefit from the seaside air. In Hove Andrew and Ruth were able to have a settled period of schooling, and Mary qualified in London as a solicitor. A weakness of the parish was that it had no church hall. But after a while, it was discovered that the back of the huge church building had only been dedicated, not consecrated. Fundraising began in earnest producing £6,000, which enabled it to be converted into a very useful hall, opened by Bishop Bell on June 24, 1956. Subsequently a 300-square-foot mural was painted on its east wall by Augustus Lunn ARCA, depicting the many facets of Sussex life. It was dedicated by the Rt. Revd. Harold E. Sexton, Archbishop of British Columbia (a father figure to Richard in his Deptford days) during his visit to England for the 1958 Lambeth Conference. In Hove Alison made looking after her family her primary role, but she also led a branch of the Mothers' Union, which, after the new hall was opened, met there. During her time in Hove, varicose veins in her legs became particularly painful and major surgery was needed. In 1958 Bishop Bell retired and died. Richard, who had been devoted to him, became restless again. His adventurous spirit and his concern for a warmer climate for the family led him to resign early in 1959, and to spend a year as Senior Chaplain to the Archbishop of Cape Town, Joost de Blanc, a former fellow student at Cambridge. Then, looking for one more major challenge, he renewed contact with the Rt. Revd. John Moyes, Bishop of Armidale in New South Wales, Australia, whom he had met in Gravesend in 1948. Bishop Moyes offered him the senior post of Archdeacon of Tamworth and Vicar of St. John's Church. He was glad to accept, and moved with his family to Tamworth in February 1960. It was in Tamworth that Alison really came into her own as a speaker. She led the Mothers' Union and soon started a Young Wives' Group. Before long, she realised the great importance of training Christian women to be devotional speakers, and began to conduct a speakers' course with the aid of a big, old tape recorder so that members of the group could hear their own trial speeches and learn to improve their style. She developed the course, repeating it several times in the parish. Diocesan records reveal that, such was her success, she was invited no less than three times during 1962-63 to speak or conduct courses on this subject in Armidale. In addition, she delivered a series of epilogues on Radio 2TM in Tamworth, and gave devotional talks at diocesan gatherings of women in Armidale and Sydney.

In 1964 Bishop Moyes retired and the next year the Daunton-Fear family moved back to England, spending a few months in Worthing before returning in 1966 to Australia to live in Adelaide. Andrew remained at Queens' College, Cambridge to complete the theological tripos for a B.A. and then follow them. Richard was appointed Organising Chaplain of the Bishop's Home Mission Society of the Diocese of Adelaide, as well as Archdeacon of Gawler, a post created especially for him. Mary took up work as a Senior Lecturer in law at the University of Adelaide, and Ruth studied history at Flinders University, while Andrew became a tutor and lecturer at Ridley College, Melbourne. Alison had no parish responsibilities but was invited to give various talks and conduct quiet days and retreats for women's groups at the Diocesan Retreat House at Belair in the hills behind Adelaide, and in some parishes of the diocese. She also gave a talk on public speaking to a group of lay-readers of the diocese. Her work continued until Richard resigned from his posts in 1970. While Mary continued to teach in Adelaide, the rest of the family spent some months in the picturesque seaside town of Tumby Bay near Port Lincoln. In September 1971 Andrew and Ruth flew back to London to take a course in librarianship. Early in 1972 Richard, Alison and Joan Apperley, who had lived with the family since Gravesend days, moved to St. Helier in Jersey, where Richard took up the post of Honorary Curate of St. Matthew's Millbrook. Though he officially retired in 1973, he continued to assist there and at other churches in Jersey. Alison was occasionally called upon to lead Bible studies and on Good Friday 1974 contributed two talks at a three-hour service at St. Martin's Parish Church. This proved to be the most settled period of their lives as they continued to live on the island until 1983. They had a little walled garden in which they grew many vegetables. Towards the end of their time in Jersey, Alison, having long suffered with acute osteo-arthritis, was admitted to St. Luke's Hospital for Clergy in London, and had both hips replaced, six months apart.

In 1983, chiefly because Jersey's airport was so often fog-bound in the colder months, making visits from the family difficult, Richard,

Alison and Joan moved to St. Austell, Cornwall. There Richard was occasionally invited to celebrate and preach in local churches, and during Holy Week 1987 Alison conducted a Quiet Day for the Women's Fellowship of St. Mewan's Parish Church. This appears to have been her last public engagement. But of special delight to them during their time in Cornwall were visits by Ruth, her husband Nigel and their young son Paul, born in 1981. After four years at St. Austell, since in reality they knew very few people in Cornwall, they moved back to Worthing in West Sussex, a town they had loved since taking their honeymoon there so long before. Their home was 38 Ladydell Road, a bungalow in the east of the town, within easy reach of shops. There they spent their last years. Richard was occasionally invited to take services and preach, but much of their time they spent in the garden, enjoying its tranquillity. After Richard died on June 9, 1993 Alison and Joan stayed on in the house. In July 1995 Mary (60) and Andrew (50) held a joint celebratory birthday dinner in Worthing for some 30 people. After the jocular speeches were over, to everyone's surprise and delight, Alison herself rose and spoke from her heart on 'What I have learnt from my children.' It was a touching moment. Sadly, within a month she began to suffer trans-ischemic attacks and no further speeches were possible. She faced her limitations with characteristic courage, dying peacefully on August 22, 2001, grateful for a long and interesting life.

Notes

[1] Children's Special Service Mission. This was the original name of the Scripture Union.

[2] Luke 9:62.

[3] The information in this paragraph comes almost entirely from the book *Ridgelands Calling!* by Christine I. Tinling (London: Marshall Morgan & Scott, 1933). For source material the author stayed for a while at the College, observing its activities, and interviewed the Principal and a number of students.

[4] The Rt. Revd. Richard Parsons.

[5] His twenty-fourth birthday.

[6] All this information comes from Mary E. Hart's *A Street Trilogy* (Street: C & J C Museum, 1995), and Street Parochial Church Council minutes.

[7] 'A Spiritual Charge to Combined Parochial Church Councils.'

[8] She had been buried in a previous church there in 1617.

[9] Alison's account of this trip is given in Appendix 1.

Notes Continued

[10] According to a contemporary report in the Gravesend and Dartford Reporter, this was £6,000. A later account in an Australian paper, drawing information surely from Richard himself, by then Archdeacon of Tamworth, states £8,500. Presumably these figures include the money donated by the Americans.

[11] An order of service and a photograph of this occasion have been preserved, and further information is found in newspaper cuttings.

[12] In the time of the next Rector, Canon Selwyn Gummer, St. George's became the parish church of Gravesend, and St. James' church was demolished.

Tributes

"With gratitude and praise, we offer ourselves, with our talents and treasure, to be messengers of your good news." This could be a prayer said by Mrs. Daunton-Fear before one of her many Training Sessions given to women parishioners in the parish of Tamworth, New South Wales. I was fortunate to be one of them, a very young clergy wife at the time, and I found her lectures inspirational, and her advice and guidance stood by me throughout the rest of my life in parish work. The warmth of her personality, together with the wisdom and guidance shared through her teaching of the Word of God and its application to our own lives, reach out to us over all those years, and are as relevant today as they were then.

Laurel Joy Lancaster
(Curate's Wife)
From an email to Andrew dated January 17, 2019

I have fond memories of both your parents and will always be thankful for their sound biblical teaching. I was a fairly new Christian when they came to St. John's, Tamworth and could not get enough of what they had to say. Your mother spent time with me instructing me on how to give a talk. She said to keep to three points and form pictures in the mind. I am sure that forming pictures in her talks presented the Bible more clearly for people. We were blessed to have both your parents speak at services. They both presented the Bible powerfully. It appears your mother found that the Mothers' Union played cards when they met together; she asked them if they would like her to read to them about the founder of Mothers' Union, Mary Sumner. I was not a member until your mother started an evening group for younger mothers. We were instructed in the importance of looking to God's Word in dealing with our husbands and rearing our children, like Mary Sumner instructed.

Daphne Wilson
From an email to Mary dated January 12, 2019
Mary is godmother of Daphne's son Mark

Not only is your mother remembered as the founder of St. John's Wives Fellowship, but she is remembered with much affection by many of us as a godly and gracious lady, who encouraged us greatly in our faith, and in our role as wives and mothers.

Fran Newling
From a letter to Ruth dated October 24, 2001,
after Ruth had informed her of Mother's death

How the years have flown! It is nearly forty years since I went to Tamworth as Curate, and I have the fondest memories of you and the family. I think of all the wonderful meals you cooked in a very hot climate, and your wonderful hospitality. Also your great spiritual strength and faith, and your leadership of the Mothers' Union and Young Wives' Fellowship. I remember one of your favourite hymns was 'Jesus, I am resting, resting in the joy of what Thou art', and in times of difficulties and pressure in ministry and personal life those words have come back to me again and again.

John Clarke
From a letter to Mother dated November 16, 1999

It has been both a joy and a privilege to me to type the notes on which my mother's devotional talks were based. They range over a long period of time – from 1934 onwards. Surprisingly these notes have only recently come to light and for me, their appearance has been like discovering a spiritual gold mine! Mother left the notes in an unpretentious folder and inside it, we found a luggage label on which she had written, "Just to show you I did not spend all my time in the kitchen! Mum."

It is now over 19 years since my mother died and yet our memories of her within the family remain strong and inspirational. Above all she was a loving wife and mother whose Christian faith radiated through her to all with whom she came into contact. We always knew that her prayer times were sacrosanct and, as far as possible, she shared our individual prayer times too, certainly when we were younger. We were also aware of her ministry mainly amongst women's groups, especially her beloved Mothers' Union. However, educational commitments frequently took each of us away from home and we rarely actually heard her speak.

Some of the talks have brought me close to tears for the sheer beauty of them. I have also become aware afresh of the reality of the presence of God for her. And as I typed, I have shared this wonderful experience too and the almost overwhelming sense of joy that comes with it. Of all the talks which came alive for me, the one on the Emmaus Road is the most memorable with those wonderful words, "Jesus himself drew near." Indeed, those words were used recurrently by my mother in widely different situations, whether to combat loneliness and isolation in rural Australia or to support the war-weary in fear of imminent invasion during the Second World War. The words are capable of universal comfort.

It is my prayer that whatever challenges readers of this little book are facing, they, too, will know the sense of peace which the presence of God can bring them. "Jesus himself drew near."

Mary

When I was a child, my mother was always a caring and encouraging presence in our home. She gladly welcomed my school friends, and when I was ill and off school with asthma or winter ailments, she would play table games with me. I remember especially Battleships and L'Attaque (despite her being a pacifist!), but I feel sure we also played noughts and crosses, snakes and ladders, and draughts. She was scrupulously fair to us children. Once when we asked her which of us she loved the most, she replied, "You all have a special place in my heart, and none can take the place of the other." End of discussion.

After a while, I noticed Mother was not around after breakfast each day, and that at these times her bedroom door was closed. One day I knocked and went in. She was sitting on her bed with a Bible open in front of her. I asked if I could stay and was told, "Yes, if you're very quiet." I stayed while she read the Bible and prayed – but never interrupted her again from that time! She had taught all of us children to say our prayers before going to bed, but here she was leading by example.

My sisters and I very seldom heard Mother give a public talk, though in Tamworth I did listen to some of her broadcast epilogues, and was once present at a Youth Fellowship variety show in the church hall in which she had been given the spiritual slot. Nothing daunted, she spoke on the Rich Young Ruler and, from start to finish, held everyone's rapt attention. I now know the secret of her power as a speaker came from her deep spiritual life, her knowledge of the Bible, her love of life and people, her enquiring mind and a certain dramatic flair. I have been awed in recent months to read the scripts of her talks and am so glad that now we can make some of them known to a wider audience.

Andrew

When we were living in London, we had a very dear friend who was an architect. He would say to us sometimes, "Look up." Very often in towns and cities there are rather plain shop fronts and, above, the most beautifully embellished original buildings. It seems to me that, in her talks, my mother often invited us to look up from our ordinary lives to the divine. She did not in any way wish to lessen the value of our ordinary lives, but to enhance them from a spiritual perspective. It can be hard for us to do this; we tend to look down. Gradually it can be part of our lives, bringing a clearer insight. My mother had clearly practised looking up throughout her life and she was a most loving, understanding and kindly person.

Ruth

Her children rise up and call her blessed.

Proverbs 31:28

Photographs

Left: Alison with her father.
Right: Alison (right) with her mother and sister.

Left: Ridgelands Bible College.
Right: Mrs Howard Hooker, Principal.

Left: Holy Trinity, Street. Right: Dora, Alison and Andrew.

Family Group in Gravesend. Back: Richard, Alison,
Winifred (Sister Anastasia), Aileen and Kenneth.
Front: Michael, Andrew, Dora, Mary and Rosemary
(Michael and Rosemary, children of Kenneth and Aileen).

Left: St. George's, Gravesend.
Right: Alison and Joan at the Pocahontas memorial.

The Archdeacon of Tamworth and family.

Alison's first speakers' class graduation.
Alison (third from left), Joan Cole, Mayoress of Tamworth
(centre), Joy Lancaster (third from right), Gloria Thew
(second from right).

Alison and Joan with Ruth, her husband Nigel and son Paul.

Alison and Joan with Mary,
her husband Charles and Jacko.

Left: Last public speech.
Right: With Helmut and Monika Wilhelm.

Family group at Mary's home.
Back: Ruth, Nigel and Andrew.
Front: Jenny (Andrew's wife) and Mary.

Early Ministry

Living Sacrifices[1]

Present your bodies a living sacrifice.

Romans 12:1

We often think of sacrifice as something coming occasionally into our lives. The great crises are times of sacrifice to God, but really God calls us not to *make* sacrifices but to *live* them – to be a living sacrifice. It is a continuous process – it does not end when we finish our prayer time or at the close of a meeting. The life of Christ was a living sacrifice. It is easier for us to bear witness with our words rather than by our lives. If we are not living sacrifices, then often our lives cancel our words. I want to tell you of two men who were 'living sacrifices'.

The first was a minister of Christ in Deptford.[2] His aim was to spend his life and to be spent for Christ. He worked amongst poverty and squalor. He sat with the sick, supported the weak and followed closely his Master who came to minister and not be ministered to.[3] Communism in Deptford was very strong at the time. The community was mixed racially with black people, white people and Chinese all living there. The Communist leader was called Nobby Clarke.[4] There were constant uprisings and brawls. Police frequently made baton charges and arrests. The Baptists openly prayed for God to save him. The minister of Christ was there among the people when one day Nobby Clarke threw a stone at his face. "Father, forgive them; for they know not what they do,"[5] prayed the minister, and his face was as the face of an angel as he looked into Nobby Clarke's eyes.[6]

Later, instead of making accusations against him, the minister went to his home and said, "Nobby, you have a poisoned finger, let me bind it up for you." At this, Nobby broke down physically and in every other way. He was broken like Saul who was haunted by the living sacrifice of Stephen and his lovely face. Although Nobby too had made havoc in the Church, he too heard the voice of Jesus Christ saying, 'Why are you persecuting me?'[7] In Nobby was born a desire to become a living sacrifice for Christ. Coster-mongers put their pennies together. They had been in fear of him, but now they paid for him to go to a Baptist College. After two years Nobby asked to go to a most difficult sphere of work. Accordingly, he was sent to the Belgian Congo and spent four years among cannibals who had no moral code whatever.[8] Two hundred

3

people were baptised into the Christian faith, one of them a tribal chief. Then Nobby's heart turned again to that one in England who had brought him to Christ, and he came home to London. But he was mentally and physically exhausted and became paralysed. He was quite helpless and was admitted to hospital. The minister of Jesus went to him in hospital and wrote on a slate, "Those who love God will look after you."

Nobby recovered and went to work as a lay-reader at the minister's church. He was beloved by the people there. He was so humble. As he grew stronger, a desire was born in him to be ordained. I shall never forget the tears which flowed after his ordination.[9] Nobby truly had 'a broken and a contrite heart'.[10] The great gift of public speaking which Nobby had used against God was taken and used with great power by God. Four years ago he sailed again, this time to South Africa, under the auspices of SPG,[11] and through his living sacrifice, many are being won for Christ. He has set up two churches for coloured people and established a 'Railway Mission'; people come to meet him at railway stations where he holds services. Holy Communion is celebrated in the waiting rooms of the stations[12] and those who attend, in their turn, are becoming living sacrifices.

I beseech you therefore, brethren, by the mercies of God, that you present your bodies a living sacrifice, holy, acceptable to God, which is your reasonable service.[13]

Notes

[1] This talk was given in 1942, but as the early incidents it relates took place in Deptford in the east end of London, where Father was a Curate in the early 1930s, it is surely fitting that it should be placed first amongst Mother's talks.

[2] Perhaps the Rev. George Henry Lunn, Vicar of St. John's Deptford, 1930-36, or indeed Alison's own husband Richard.

[3] Mark 10:45.

[4] 'Nobby' was a nickname given sometimes to people with the surname 'Clark(e)'; its origin is uncertain. This man's full name was George Robert Clarke.

[5] Luke 23:34.

[6] cf. Acts 6:15 (Stephen).

[7] Acts 9:4.

Notes Continued

8   It is clear the Baptist Missionary Society had missionaries in the Belgian Congo at this time, including Clement Clapton Chesterton who was a medical missionary at Yakusu, 1920-36 (Wikipedia). Cannibalism was well-known in the Congo, combatted more effectively by Christian missions than by the Belgian authorities (see William F. P. Burton, *Congo Sketches*, London: Victory Press, c.1950, pp. 1, 49-51). Sexual unfaithfulness was characteristic of a society where chiefs practised gross polygamy (see Norman Grubb, *Christ in Congo Forests: The Story of the Heart of Africa Mission*, London: Lutterworth, 1945, pp. 59-63, 100).

9   He was ordained deacon in 1938 in Chichester for ministry in the Diocese of George, South Africa, and priest in the Diocese of George in 1939.

10   Psalm 51:17.

11   The Society for the Propagation of the Gospel, now called United Society Partners in the Gospel. In the USPG archives in the Bodleian Library in Oxford there is a letter from "G. R. Clarke" to the Revd. W. F. France at 15 Tufton Street, Westminster SW1 (SPG headquarters), dated March 22, 1938, in which he says he intends to sail for South Africa on the Grantully Castle on May 6 with his wife Martha and young daughters Brenda Grace and Evelyn Doris. Subsequent letters from the Chief Accountant of the SPG to the Bishop of George tell of donations for Mr. Clarke's stipend from Lindfield (1940) and Street (1941, 1943). These surely imply continuing contact with the Daunton-Fear family.

12   The South African Church Railway Mission was founded in 1902 and continued until 1980. Its Constitution states as its object: "To carry the ministration of the Church to those who live along the South African Railways ... and are out of reach of the normal work of the parochial clergy, by means of chaplains and workers who shall make the Railway employees and their families their first care..." Crockford Clerical Directory says that George Robert Clarke was Curate of St. Jude's Oudtshoorn (Eastern Cape), 1938-46. There was a railway station at Oudtshoorn, so Nobby Clarke's railway mission would seem to have been thereabouts.

13   Romans 12:1

Christ in Ordinary Things

He was known to them in the breaking of bread.

Luke 24:35

Sometimes we feel that if we were especially talented or rich, we would be of more use in the world. We are very ordinary people, doing ordinary things – cooking, cleaning, darning and shopping – and we feel we would like to do something out of the ordinary. If only I could climb a mountain peak or walk on water or do something extraordinary!

The incident on the Emmaus Road[1] is an exquisite story of a man and his wife. Jesus was unrecognisable on the journey but suddenly, "He was known to them in the breaking of bread." They invited him in to a simple evening meal when it was getting dark, and as he sat down, they asked him to say grace. He took bread and blessed it and broke it and gave it to them, and their eyes were opened and they knew him. He was known to them in just this simple act, something familiar to all of us. It was always this way. He came to people and was known to them in the simple things – in considering the lilies, in considering the seeds, the vine, the water.

I come in little things,
Saith the Lord:
Not borne on morning wings
Of majesty, but I have set my feet
Amidst the delicate and bladed wheat
That springs triumphant in the furrowed sod –
There do I dwell in weakness and in power;
Not broken or divided, saith our God!
In your strait garden plot I come to flower:
About your porch my vine
Meek, fruitful doth entwine;
Waits at the threshold, Love's appointed hour.

I come in the little things,
Saith the Lord;
Yea! on the glancing wings
Of eager birds, the softly pattering feet
Of furred and gentle beasts, I come to meet
Your hard and wayward heart. In brown bright eyes

That peep from out the woods, I stand confest.
On every nest
Where feathery Patience is content to brood
And leaves her pleasure for the high emprise
Of motherhood –
There does my Godhead rest.

I come in the little things,
Saith the Lord;
My starry wings
I do forsake,
Love's highway of humility to take;
Meekly I fit my stature to your need.
In beggar's part
About your gates I shall not cease to plead –
As man, to speak with man –
Till by such art
I shall achieve my immemorial plan,
Pass the low lintel of the human heart.[2]

Yes, he could have come in the thunder but he came in the still, small voice. He could have come as a prince but he came as a poor working man. He could have come as a king in costly raiment but he came as a little baby in a manger for his cradle.

We do not need to seek him away from the ordinary things. "He was known to them in the breaking of bread." He can be known to us in gentleness, in meekness, in a simple act. The bread of our meals can be a sacrament of his presence, the sacrament of our Holy Communion. He transforms the ordinary not by changing it but by *taking* it. Although we ourselves are ordinary, he can take the bread of our lives into his hands. He does not take by force. On the Emmaus Road, he was *invited in* to take bread. This is always the order for our lives. "He took bread and blessed it."[3] We can only be blessed as we are taken by him. And after that he "broke and gave it to them". And before our lives can be given to help others, they must be broken in his hands – the breaking of a wayward heart.

We need more broken hearts because our hearts are proud and selfish and self-righteous. And when the common bread of our lives is taken in his hands and blessed and broken, then it can be given to nourish and sustain others. We are all broken differently; for some it is by bereavement, for others it is by hardship or illness. Always remember that our sins broke him first. "This is my body which is broken for you."[4] We are only broken by One who knows to the fullest extent what breaking means.

Notes

1. Luke 24:13-35.
2. 'Immanence', by Evelyn Underhill (1912). Here in stanza 2, line 7, "woods" replaces the unfamiliar "brake".
3. Luke 24:30.
4. 1 Corinthians 11:24.

Getting Back in Touch with God

If I may touch but the hem of his garment.

And Jesus said, somebody touched me for I perceive that virtue is gone out of me.

Matthew 9:20-21, Luke 8:46 (KJV)

There are two kinds of people that we meet today:

- those who are quite out of touch with God;
- those who are in close touch with God.

The people belonging to the first group have no spiritual understanding. They are purely materialistic in their outlook. They live within the tiny limited circle of their own self-wills. They live for what they can get out of this world in money and comfort. Their appetites are well satisfied. They have a moral code but make sure that it is not too exacting a one! They live entirely for themselves.

There are others in this group too – those who once were in touch with God and who have lost touch. Most of us have lost touch at some time in our lives, when we have given ourselves up to worldly pursuits. It is a desolate experience. The worst thing that can happen to a soul is to lose consciousness of God's presence. We wander then in a dry and thirsty land. Perhaps we were brought into touch with Jesus Christ at a mission, or a service, or at work, or at home, and we realised that spiritual values are the only lasting values in life. Since then someone or something has come between us and God. Perhaps the influence of a friend attracted us away and we lost touch. We have not kept the vows we made to God. Prayer has been difficult and so we have lost the touch we once had with spiritual powers and we find ourselves with no reserve of strength when our own is spent. It is like the loss of power in a limb – we lose the use of our lives and limbs and mind for God. How can we be restored to that close touch with our Lord?

The *first step* comes when we know and recognise our need of God's touch upon us. A young married couple said, "We realised the need of a Power outside ourselves." If we are self-confident and self-sufficient we haven't taken the first step. Revelation 3:17 shows the warning given to the Laodicean church: "Because you say, I am rich, have become wealthy, *and have need of nothing* – and do not know that you are wretched, miserable, poor, blind and naked…" We need a divine dissatisfaction with ourselves. Instead of measuring ourselves very favourably beside the stunted growth of human nature, we should measure ourselves beside the fullness of the stature of Christ and see how short we are of his perfection.

Let us watch someone else who was taking this *first step* of coming into touch with our Lord. She was a woman of infirmity, for "she had suffered many things of many doctors":[1]

- she had tapped many sources and had spent all she had;
- she was a pauper.

Sometimes we live on our spiritual capital instead of having a spiritual income, and we find we have spent all and have not become better but rather grown worse. This woman, knowing the hopelessness of her condition, summoned up all her faith and took the *second step*, going towards Jesus in the midst of the crowd. It was the step of faith, "If I may touch but the hem of his garment I shall be made whole."

The hem of his garment is within our reach – that which we can most easily grasp – the hem of God's salvation reaching down in Jesus, within the reach of a child. Perhaps we have seen just the edge of spiritual truth, some tangible evidence of his presence. Grasp the hem of his garment – as a child learning to walk holds the hem of its mother's dress. Grasp the hem that you can reach knowing that there are higher reaches. Above the hem is the heart and mind of God. He will soon lift you up to reach up higher.

The result of the woman's touch with God was a *new power*. She felt in her body that she was healed. "And Jesus immediately knew in himself that virtue had gone out of him." The Greek for "virtue" here is *dynamis*, 'power'. It is a transforming power that is released by our touch with him, power that goes out from God to man. It is a power that reaches down to the hidden root of the trouble, that heals the cause and not the symptom.

Our modern psychologists try to do that and fail, but we read in Scripture, "Your sins are forgiven." "Go into the peace of forgiveness."[2] It is the touch of God that sets the common bush on fire,[3] that makes of the common clay a healing balm.[4]

There must be personal contact with our Saviour and then confession and witness of our contact. It wasn't the crowd that touched him but one woman. Jesus asked, "Who touched me?" He knew who it was but wanted her confession of faith. That is the *third step* in our touch with God: "She came and fell down before him in front of them all."[5]

Notes

1   cf. Mark 5:26.

2   Luke 7:48, 50; the Greek actually says, "Go *into* peace," though our English versions do not reveal this.

3   Exodus 3.

4   John 9:6.

5   cf. Luke 8:47.

On Eagle's Wings

They that wait upon the Lord shall renew their strength; they shall mount up with wings as eagles; they shall run and not be weary; and they shall walk and not faint.

Isaiah 40:31 (KJV)

We have come here because we believe in the power of prayer. We believe that 'more things are wrought by prayer than this world dreams of.'[1] We read of the disciples, that it was *after they had prayed* that the place where they were was shaken and the Holy Spirit came upon them.[2] It is through prayer that the strongholds of Satan are shaken in the world today. Would you do the best service for the world today? Then pray for the world. Would you render the best service to our country? Then pray for it. The power of God starts to operate when we start to pray. God waited for St. Paul to be ready for his use. When he saw he was ready he said to Ananias, "Behold, he is praying."[3] When God sees us on our knees, then he can use us.

"They that wait upon the Lord shall renew their strength." If ever we wanted our strength renewed it is today; our strength is being drained by such a complicated way of living. It produces strain. When we lose strength physically, only one thing will renew it and that is rest and sleep. When we lose strength spiritually, there is only one way of restoring it, and that is by resting in God and in his strength – in waiting on the Lord. What sleep and rest are in restoring the body, so prayer is in restoring the soul.

There is so much in life today to destroy our quietness, yet we know that "in quietness and confidence shall be your strength".[4] As the popular negro spiritual urges: "Steal away, steal away to Jesus, steal away home." Three things are promised us if we "wait upon the Lord":

1) *We shall mount up with wings as eagles.* We are not speaking of sparrows' wings, or those of doves, but the wings of *eagles*, the king of birds – the birds that inhabit the mountain heights; the birds that soar nearest to the sun; the eagle that bears its young when they learn to fly by flying beneath them.[5] When we wait upon the Lord, he gives us strength to rise above our difficulties, to surmount them so that they shall not smother us. And God will also do that for those for whom we pray today.

2) *We shall run and not be weary.* We shall be able to meet all those sudden demands made upon all of us in life, the crises, the service we render to God.

3) *We shall walk and not faint.* That means just the ordinary, humdrum tasks of everyday life – the ordinary work and cares of each day, the daily *walk*, more tedious and monotonous than flying and running.

Our walking without fainting, and our running without being weary, only come after we have learned to mount up with wings as eagles. And our mounting up depends upon our waiting upon the Lord.

Notes

[1] Alfred Lord Tennyson.

[2] Acts 1:14, 2:4.

[3] Acts 9:11.

[4] Isaiah 30:15.

[5] cf. Deuteronomy 32:11. Ornithological observation in recent years has not confirmed this claim; for one thing the mature fledgling is much too heavy to be carried by its parent, but an eagle's parental concern for its offspring making its maiden flight by flying quite nearby has been noted.

An Easter Message

If Christ be not risen from the dead, then is our preaching vain and your faith is also vain.

1 Corinthians 15:14 (KJV)

In Dr. F. W. Boreham's essay 'The Rainbow' he observes that with our limited vision, we can only see the half circle. In reality, there is a whole circle.[1] As we think together of the meaning of Easter, we see that the resurrection of Christ pushes back the boundaries of our lives to encompass the whole circle. Life is never completed in this life.

Familiarity has dimmed the sharp outlines of the gospel narrative for us. Imagine the impact of the resurrection on the people who had just witnessed Calvary. There was no radiant certainty of immortality in the old Greek and Hebrew writings. The Greeks struck a note of great pathos.[2] Plato and Socrates "held that the best that man can do is to make a raft out of such materials as reason gives and drift out into the darkness".[3]

To the Hebrew seers, immortality was expressed in the word *sheol* a place of darkness and gloom, silence and an eerie ghostliness.[4] If we search the Old Testament we will find little taught about immortality except in Psalm 23. It was the experience of Easter when our Lord showed himself alive to a great many people, including 500 at once,[5] and revealed his identity by showing the scars on his hands and feet to those incredulous ones,[6] that established the joyful certainty for us all of life beyond the grave.

One of the most vital things about the resurrection was that it vindicated Christ and all his claims of divinity. The resurrection has been called the touchstone of Christianity. Without it, our Lord's death might not have differed from the death of any other martyr. The accusation against him was one of blasphemy (Matthew 27:39-44). Without the resurrection, his accusers would have been right in calling him an impostor.

Was Christ's offering on the Cross in vain? In 1 Corinthians 15:17, we read, "If Christ is not risen, your faith is futile; you are still in your sins!" Immediately following the dreadful accusations against him, darkness came upon the whole land. During that physical, mental and spiritual darkness, the spotless Son of God made his supreme offering of love. He was the Lamb of God that takes away the sins of the world.[7] We read that, in the moment of this supreme offering of his life, the veil of the Temple was torn from top to bottom,[8] the veil that had always hung between the Holy Place and the Holy of Holies. Thus, he opened up the way to God and gave us all access by faith.

> *Look, Father, look on his anointed face,*
> *And only look on us as found in him,*
> *Look not on our misusings of his grace,*
> *Our prayer so languid and our faith so dim.*
> *For lo, between our sins and their reward*
> *We set the passion of Thy Son, Our Lord.[9]*

His life and his death were completely vindicated by his resurrection. And it is not a matter of what *we can do*, but the acceptance of what *he has done*.

Notes

[1] The Rev. Dr. Frank William Boreham, OBE (1871-1959) was a renowned Baptist preacher and essayist. Though he was born in England, most of his ministry was in Australia and New Zealand. He published some 50 books of essays and sermons.

[2] In popular Greek thought, the souls of the dead were believed to be taken to Hades. It was common to place money in their mouths to pay Charon, the boatman, for the ferry ride across the River Styx. As depicted by Homer, there they were "pathetic in their helplessness, inhabiting draughty, echoing halls, deprived of their wits, and flitting purposelessly about uttering batlike noises (*Od.* 24.5ff)". ('Death, attitudes to' in *The Oxford Classical Dictionary,* 4th edn., ed. by Simon Hornblower and Antony Spawforth, Oxford University Press, 2012)

[3] It is not known who is being quoted here. According to *The Oxford Classical Dictionary*, Socrates was probably agnostic about whether the soul would survive death, but Plato believed both in the immortality of the soul (a person's life-force, intellect and personality) and in reincarnation – see its articles on 'Soul' and 'Plato'.

[4] See for instance Psalm 88.

[5] 1 Corinthians 15:6.

[6] Luke 24:39, cf. John 20:27.

[7] John 1:29.

[8] Mark 15:38.

[9] From the hymn 'And now, O Father, mindful of the love', by William Bright (1874).

Harvest Festival

There are three great necessities in the growing of our crops:
the seed – the soil – the seasons.

THE SEED

It is the germ of life that God alone can create. Science can do most things but it cannot create the germ of life. The seed must be sown. It is no use keeping seeds in a packet in a drawer; they must be sown in soil. The seed and the soil working together produce growth. God and man, seed and soil. Each are essential to the other.

THE SOIL

This needs preparation and God leaves that to man. He leaves the digging, the trenching, the weeding and the ploughing to us. The ordinary soil of our lives needs preparation to receive the good seed of God which will produce the life of God in us. The Great Sower of the good seed looks down into our hearts, searching for the right kind of soil in which to sow his seed. He seeks the soil in which his life can flourish. He sees different kinds of soil:

1) *The unprepared soil.* This is the wayside; it is hard and unbroken on the surface. It represents those who hear the word only and then the devil snatches it away.
2) *The badly prepared soil.* Here there are rocks and thorns. Where there is no depth of soil, it allows no roots. This represents those who make a superficial profession of faith. They are alright until the hot sun of adversity burns it and then it is scorched and dies because there is no depth to their faith.

   In badly prepared soil the seed also falls among weeds and thorns and gets choked and overgrown. Jesus said it gets choked by the overgrowth of cares and pleasure and riches, and there is no room for it to breathe.[1]
3) *The good soil.* This represents the prepared heart, broken and allowing room for the seed to grow – "A broken and a contrite heart … you will not despise."[2]

These are the third essential for our crops. The seed, the germ of life sown in the soil, is dependent now upon the seasons. We have to acknowledge our dependence upon the Creator for the seasons. They are constant proof of his faithfulness. In Genesis 8:22 we read, "While the earth remains, seedtime and harvest, cold and heat, winter and summer, and day and night shall not cease."

The seasons mean varying quantities of heat and cold, of rain and frost. We must have our seasons in life – not all sunshine. The cold winds of adversity and the rains of sorrow are as necessary to our growth as the sun. The high winds prune the branches of the trees. God does not leave us alone in our preparation of the soil. The process goes on all the winter, even when we see nothing, no results at all. God knows the best for us. The frosts break up the soil and act as a powerful antiseptic, killing all pests. There are things in us which need the frost to purify us. Some flowers won't grow except on a north wall.

God's seed – our soil – God's seasons.

Notes

[1] Mark 4:19.

[2] Psalm 51:17.

War and Peace

After the Fall of Paris and France[1]

Those Cheddar caves! It is said it takes one million years for one inch of rock to form.[2] What ageless rock! How short is our lifespan in comparison! Centuries ago people were looking at the same rocks. And in centuries to come, whatever the outcome of this war, people will still look and marvel at the rocks. It steadies one. They will remain the same, though more geological information may be discovered about them. The fact that man did not discover those caves in the rock does not mean they were not there. They have been there for millions of years.

In Isaiah 32:2 we read, "A man will be as a hiding place from the wind, and a cover from the tempest; rivers of water in a dry place, as the shadow of a great rock in a weary land." Could anything be more weary than our land at the moment? There is not only physical but mental weariness, emotional weariness – nerve strain. That is because some of us have lived like the people 100 years ago in Cheddar – that underground great shelter and beauty of rock was there all the time but not discovered![3]

It reminds one of John the Baptist's cry, "There stands one among you whom you do not know."[4] He still stands as the eternal rock of ages in a weary land. Have we discovered him wholly? "I am Alpha and Omega ... Heaven and earth shall pass away *but my word shall endure for ever.*"[5] Things are passing away from us. Things and governments change overnight. "Change and decay in all around I see: O Thou who changest not, abide with me."[6]

In Hebrews 1:11 we read, "They shall perish but you remain." It may well be that in these days all material things are being shaken, so that we may at last discover those things that cannot be shaken. "Now abide faith, hope and love."[7] In the face of death, in the face of loss, national and physical, all true values remain for us in Jesus, the same yesterday, today and forever.[8] Is a difference apparent in Christians so that others may know that we cannot be shaken?

Isaiah 32:2 speaks of a desert experience, the need for shelter, rest and refreshment from the blazing sun. We need not be ashamed of our need for rest. We cannot go on physically and spiritually without it. No armies can fight, no housewives work without rest and shelter. A great deal is being done for the shelter of our bodies in air raids. As Christians, we should also seek shelter for our souls and 'fear not them which can kill the body'.[9]

Jesus is our Rock in a weary land. He provides:

1) *Shelter from the wind,* which in a desert whips up the sand and bits of grit. These are the small annoyances we face. Take them into his presence.
2) *Shelter from the tempest,* which creates a danger of being swept away – by war. "Rock of ages cleft for me, let me hide myself in Thee."[10]
3) *Rivers of water in a dry place.* Major Simson spoke of the value of prayer in the dry place of battle. We can pray during an air raid.
4) *Shade from the sun.* We must protect our faith from being burnt and destroyed.

Lastly, we are told not just to snatch shelter but to *build* on the rock. "Dear Name, the rock on which I build, my shield and hiding place..."[11] In Matthew 7:24-27 we read:

> *Whoever hears these sayings of mine, and does them, I will liken him to a wise man who built his house on the rock: and the rain descended, the floods came, and the winds blew and beat on that house; and it did not fall, for it was founded on the rock. But everyone who hears these sayings of mine, and does not do them, will be like a foolish man who built his house on the sand: and the rain descended, the floods came and the winds blew and beat on that house; and it fell, and great was its fall.*

We build, not by knowing or listening, but *by doing* what Jesus tells us. He speaks of a home built on a rock. Is our home built there?

Notes

1 Paris fell on June 14, 1940, and the French surrendered to the Germans on June 18.
2 Should this be "a thousand years"? Perhaps, but bear in mind this present-day statement: "The formation and development of caves is known as speleogenesis, which can occur over the course of millions of years." (Wikipedia, 'Cave')
3 Gough's cave, a very popular tourist attraction today, was not excavated until the 1890s, and later opened to the public; in it were found human remains from c. 9,000 years ago.

Notes Continued

4 John 1:26.

5 cf. Revelation 22:13, Matthew 24:35 (KJV).

6 From the hymn 'Abide with me', by Henry Francis Lyte (1847).

7 1 Corinthians 13:13.

8 Hebrews 13:8.

9 Matthew 10:28.

10 Hymn by Augustus Montague Toplady (1763).

11 From the hymn 'How sweet the name of Jesus sounds', by John Newton (1779).

Jesus Himself Drew Near

Luke 24:15

We are always having to face the unknown. We never tread the same path again – we always have to break fresh ground, every day, every tomorrow. We wish it were not so because we love the old familiar paths and landmarks. Yet time marches on. We have only trodden down two months of the present New Year. What were your feelings? There was grotesque dancing down the bombed streets of London.[1] Those who felt the solemnity of the New Year did not dance but prayed it in with trembling hearts. Impending invasion and danger are talked of today. Before the war we had put much faith in our prayers for peace and they failed. Up to the last moment we had hoped that God would avert the tragedy of war. Our hopes were dashed. Instead of God's intervention we are left with relentless suffering and destruction. With these thoughts pushed to the back of our minds, we face a new unknown road of tomorrow.

Yet we are not alone. We read in Luke 24 of two others who faced a new unknown road with the same feelings; probably they were husband and wife. The road stretched from Jerusalem to Emmaus. They had had great hopes and faith in Christ. They knew with certainty that he was a prophet mighty in deed and word before God. Their faith in him had been so strong that up to the last they trusted he would redeem their nation – save them nationally. They prayed that he would save them but he couldn't even save himself. He was overpowered and destroyed and crucified. In their hearts still rang the cry of a forsaken man: "My God, my God, why have you forsaken me?"[2]

Then Jesus himself drew near and went with them and they found that they were not travelling alone. They thought he was destroyed and powerless, that evil had conquered, that he had left them alone. Some of us have been tempted to feel the same. Is he aloof and untouched by our suffering? It is just then, in that place of hopelessness, that he is near. This is the message of strength given us to help us face the future. Not that he sends us out alone but that he goes with us – into danger, into suffering and into disappointment. It was in the furnace of trial and persecution that the fourth man was seen by Daniel to be "like the Son of God".[3]

But on the Emmaus Road their eyes were restrained and they did not recognise him. We often live as if we had no recognition of him. What are the factors that restrain our eyes like theirs? I believe there are three:

1) *Preoccupation with the events of the day.* On the Emmaus Road they could not see beyond these.
2) *Self-pity and self-centredness.* They felt so sorry for themselves.
3) *Unbelief.* They were "slow of heart" to believe.

At first the disciples talked together and tried to reason it all out. Then they let Jesus talk to them. They gradually took him into their confidence, so much so that they constrained him to come into their home and, in that intimate confidence of the family circle over an evening meal, he said grace; then they recognised him – their eyes were opened. Their attention centred on him and not on themselves.

Recognition of his presence in our homes and daily life is the key to the future. General Gordon[4] told the story of a little boy who was lost and cried out to his father, "Is your face towards me?" God's face is always towards us, it is only our faces that turn away. The Duchess of Somerset[5] tells us, "Live as if he is there and you will find him there."

Recognition began to dawn on the disciples when Jesus opened to them the Scriptures. One of the ways he draws near to us is through the Bible. Read it to your children. I always make some time quiet in the day.

Recognise his constant presence by talking to him as the disciples talked. Brother Lawrence in *The Practice of the Presence of God* said, "Special prayer time to me is no different from any other time of day."[6] Only by *our* recognition of Jesus in our homes will our children learn to recognise him. Teach them that talking to him is as natural as talking to each other. They are not self-conscious. Pray with them over difficulties. Have we no time? As long as we have time to breathe, we have time to pray. Jesus himself drew near and went with them. May our eyes not be restrained so that we do not recognise him.

Notes

[1] Was this during 'the Blitz', September 1940 - May 1941, when one third of London was destroyed?
[2] Matthew 27:46 (Psalm 22:1).
[3] Daniel 3:25.
[4] Presumably General George Charles Gordon (1833-1885).

Notes Continued

⁵ Perhaps this was Frances Seymour (1699-1754), wife of the 7th Duke of Somerset, who was a poet, literary patron and woman of letters. She wrote some religious poems, corresponded with the influential early Methodist Selina, Countess of Huntingdon, and had among her protégés Isaac Watts, Dissenting minister and hymn-writer, author of 'When I survey the wondrous cross'.

⁶ Second conversation with M. Beaufort (17th century).

Treasure in Heaven

Provide yourselves ... a treasure in the heavens that does not fail.

Luke 12:33

We are very often reminded of our national treasures at the moment because they are in such danger of destruction – treasures like our great cathedrals, our monuments and our art galleries. One good thing is that we really begin to value our treasures when they are threatened. In our childhoods, we have read books about buried treasure – books like *Treasure Island*[1] and *Treasure Trove.*[2] Precious things are likely to be stolen.

What about the safety of our own treasures? We all have them – not costly things, but our treasures all the same – a picture, a book, a piece of china, a vase. They call to memory someone dearly loved, some hallowed place of our marriage, some song, some day. I wonder how many of us have kept some treasure belonging to our first baby – little garments or a toy. I don't suppose anyone else knows they are there but ourselves. We cling to these things and say, "I wouldn't lose them for all the world." And yet today we are facing losing material treasures which can never be replaced. How difficult it is for those having to abandon their homes to know which of their treasures to save! We are being brought face to face with our life's true values. People crossing the oceans have to be prepared day and night to leave the ship at a second's notice. A friend has said to me, "It is strange to realise the few things which are of real value to me – a Bible, my wife's ring, a passport. Nothing else."

When we examine our treasures, we find that real treasure is a person and the things associated with that person. Someone beloved. Jesus said, "Where your treasure is there is your heart also."[3] Provide yourselves treasure in heaven.[4] Love is the only treasure which cannot be destroyed. Love is eternal and immortal, and no thieves can break through and steal it from us.

We are told that Mary the mother of Jesus had this treasure of love in her heart. She kept the angels' song and the shepherds' adoration in her heart and she treasured them there.[5] She treasured the cradle even when it became a cross. How can *we* lay up for ourselves our treasures in heaven where neither moth nor rust corrupts? We want them to be stored in a place of safety.

At Christmas we are told that they brought their treasures to him.[6] We must learn to bring our treasures – our loved ones – to him too. We must surrender them to his safekeeping. We must give up our right of possession. Jesus said to the rich ruler, "Give up your possessions ... sell them ... and you will have treasure in heaven."[7] When we give our treasures to Jesus, he often gives them back. In bringing him our treasures, we bring him our hearts and we find more and more of that treasure that does not fail. In him are hidden all the treasures of wisdom and knowledge[8] – more than have ever been discovered: treasures of love, of beauty, of gentleness and forgiveness – all that is most precious to our lives.

Notes

[1]   Robert Louis Stevenson (1883).
[2]   Possibly *Treasure Trove of Pirate Stories*, ed. Ramon Wilke Kessler (1930).
[3]   cf. Matthew 6:21.
[4]   cf. Matthew 6:20.
[5]   Luke 2:19.
[6]   Matthew 2:11.
[7]   cf. Luke 18:22.
[8]   Colossians 2:3.

Liberty through the Spirit

Where the Spirit of the Lord is, there is liberty.

2 Corinthians 3:17

Let me begin by reminding you of two well-known facts:

1) the Unknown Warrior's grave[1] became a symbol of efforts to secure the liberty of the world;
2) liberty is painted in political speeches as Utopia.

Freedom as such is not all that it seems. There is always a danger it may become licence. What we need is the right use of freedom. A statesman in America has said, "The essential condition for any lasting peace is a New Spirit. The battle for peace must be fought in the heart of the individual, it necessitates a change of heart."

Admiral Byrd, the Antarctic Explorer, has said, "I went exploring because I was fired by those pioneers of history who feel the urge of charting uncharted seas and discovering unknown places. However today in this crisis which threatens to destroy freedom and civilization, the most important pioneering to be done is in the realm of the spirit."[2]

THIS PROBLEM OF FREEDOM IS A SPIRITUAL PROBLEM

We can only find the quality of spirit that will secure true liberty in our Lord Jesus Christ. He came into a world already in bondage, and in the synagogue he made a proclamation of liberty. In St. Luke's Gospel 4:18-19 we read he said:

> *The Spirit of the Lord is upon me because he has anointed me to preach the gospel to the poor; he has sent me to heal the brokenhearted, to proclaim liberty to the captives and recovery of sight to the blind, to set at liberty those who are oppressed; to proclaim the acceptable year of the Lord.*

And we are told that the eyes of all in the synagogue were fastened upon him. That is where we must fasten our eyes too, not on the terrors of this present time. What holds our gaze today?

TO FIND LIBERTY WE MUST SEE JESUS

In 2 Corinthians 4:6 we read: "For ... God ... has shone in our hearts to give the light of the knowledge of the glory of God in the face of Jesus

Christ." A small child said to his grandmother, "Nanny, I wish God had a face!" Men and women looking into the face of Jesus found true liberty – freedom from the inner bondage of a sinful heart. Jesus found:

- *The poor in bondage to the rich.* He gave the Gospel to the poor.
- *Broken hearts in bondage to self-pity.* He healed them.
- *Men and women made the captives of self.* He gave deliverance.
- *People in bondage to intellectual doubts.* He recovered their spiritual sight.
- *Lives bruised by faithlessness and impurity.* He restored to them pure hearts by his forgiveness and cleansing and set them at liberty.

When they came for physical healing, he saw their bondage was deeper, a bondage of heart and will. Jesus said, "Your sins are forgiven you."[3]

HE ALWAYS REDUCED SOCIAL PROBLEMS TO THE PERSONAL PROBLEM

People in the world today are still seeking his Spirit. God made provision for the world to be supplied by his Spirit through individuals. The lack of liberty amongst nations is only in proportion to the lack of his Spirit in individuals. In other words, freedom is limited because we have limited his Spirit. He did not mean his life merely to be an *example* but an *experience:* "You shall receive power when the Holy Spirit has come upon you."[4]

- First, we must *see* our Saviour. In 2 Corinthians 3:18 we read: "We all, with unveiled face, beholding as in a mirror the glory of the Lord..."
- Secondly, we must be *changed* by him (the verse continues): "...are being transformed into the same image from glory to glory, just as by the Spirit of the Lord" – not by our own fruitless effort. Neither will the world be changed by its own effort but by his Spirit. Jesus never left anyone the same.

We find wonderful examples in Confucius and in the Buddha but they could not transfer their lives to their disciples. At Pentecost the life of Jesus passed into his body, the Church. The disciples were changed into the same image by his Spirit. The divine fellowship formed many flames but there was only one fire. In that fellowship, we see men of great and glorious liberty. This is what Jesus meant in Luke 12:49-50 when he said, "I came to send fire on the earth ... and how distressed I am till it is accomplished." He is still distressed, but "where the Spirit of the Lord is there is liberty" – in Christians?

Don't let us leave our own thoughts of the Holy Spirit till Whitsun. Receive the Holy Spirit now. "Make me a captive, Lord, and then I shall be free."[5] Let his Spirit captivate us.

Notes

[1] The body of an unknown British soldier was buried in a special grave in Westminster Abbey at a state funeral on November 11, 1920 to commemorate all who had died unknown for king and country in the Great War, 1914-1918.

[2] Rear Admiral Richard Evelyn Byrd Jr. (1888-1957) was an American naval officer and explorer, who claimed to be the first to reach both the North and South Poles, but the former claim has been disputed. (See article in Wikipedia.)

[3] Matthew 9:5.

[4] Acts 1:8.

[5] From the hymn by George Matheson (1890).

Victory through Faith

This is the victory that has overcome the world – our faith.

1 John 5:4

We often feel and live as though we had no assurance of victory in the world – as if the powers of evil and darkness were swamping all the good in the world. We see no end to suffering. These words of St. John were written to little Christian communities in cities and towns of the Roman Empire. Churches were formed by humble men and women of little or no wealth. There were great persecutions and thousands were put to death. Society was tolerating great evils. To all appearances, the power of Rome was irresistible. This was the world as John knew it and yet he had the sublime audacity to say he knew a greater power than evil: "This is the victory that has overcome the world – our faith."

In all his writings John speaks of victorious power overcoming a mighty, perpetual opposing force. The Bible is true to human experience in that it does not hide the fact that a Christian must have conflict. There is no promise of immunity from struggle but only from defeat. And we are told not to underrate the strength of the enemy. We often do. We think of our enemy in terms of flesh and blood but in Ephesians 6:12, we are told that: "We wrestle not against flesh and blood, but against principalities, against powers, against the rulers of darkness of this world, against spiritual wickedness in high places."[1] This enemy is described in the Bible as "the world". Bishop Gore[2] spoke of it as "society organised without reference to God". Materialism sets store on things visible, earthly, sexual and temporal and, of course, there is unbelief in God. Having faced our enemy squarely, God puts into our hand his secret weapon – the only way to victory – faith.

"This is the victory – even our *faith*." Faith does not depend on physical sight. Faith is divine *second* sight. "We look not at the things which are seen, but at the things that are not seen: for the things which are seen are temporal; but the things which are not seen are eternal."[3] The Christian does not refuse to see material things *but he sees beyond them.* When the Titanic was sailing to Canada, there was a treacherous fog. However, an engineer said there was a camera with a lens that would pierce the fog. Faith is the powerful lens given us by God to pierce the mists of this world.

All our Christian martyrs have overcome the world by faith, by their power to see beyond seeming defeat, by divine second sight. Stephen, in the midst of his stoning, did not see defeat; he only saw the heavens opened and God's ultimate victory. He, being full of the Holy Ghost, looked up steadfastly into heaven and saw the glory of God and Jesus and he said, "Behold, I see the heavens opened, and the Son of Man standing on the right hand of God."[4] Can you share that vision? If we want to see the victory of faith, read Hebrews 11. This chapter is one of God's war memorials. Amongst those remembered is Moses: "By faith Moses chose rather to suffer affliction with the people of God than to enjoy the pleasures of sin."[5] Why did he make this decision? He endured as seeing him who is invisible. Can I? Can you? Can we endure the big tests as well as the trivial things?

This is the victory that overcomes the world – that is certain to prevail – even our faith in Jesus Christ. An essay on mountaineering tells of men climbing a mountain to see the sunrise only to find they are enveloped in mist, cold and damp. They returned chilled and disappointed. Yet the sun *had* risen! I can see another group of men and women enveloped in the coldest of all mists – the mists of doubt. Their hopes were shattered by the crucifixion. Yet the Son of God *had risen!* And John, remembering his resurrection and his ascension, was fired with the vision of the victorious Christ, undefeated by death and the world, unharmed and with his throne set in heaven.

When the mists of doubt close in upon us, it does not alter the *fact* of our faith – the ascended and glorified Jesus. The Son has risen. Yet the mists of doubt often chill us and it might be said more truly of us, "This is the victory that overcomes us, even our doubt!" If we are not overcoming the world by faith, the world is overcoming us. It is not surprising that the world is overcoming so much now because there is such a severe lack of faith. The world is very subtle – it makes a great appeal to us and it is so easy to accept the world's standards and become materialists. The world overcomes us when we are tired, worn out by illness, loss or war. We so easily compromise.

Are we being overcome by the world, or is the world being overcome by our faith? Jesus can overcome the world in me. The question is not, do we possess faith, but are we being possessed *by* our faith – by Jesus Christ? If we are to keep the world at bay, he must possess our hearts and wills and bodies. He alone remains untarnished by the world: "The ruler of this world ... has nothing in me."[6] "Be of good cheer, I am the vanquisher; I have overcome the world."[7] John said of the martyrs, "They overcame ... by the blood of the Lamb.'[8] His cross is our redemption. The sword of faith is in the shape of a cross. As a favourite hymn reminds us:

> *And when the strife is fierce, the warfare long,*
> *Steals on the ear the distant triumph-song,*
> *And hearts are brave again and arms are strong*
> *Alleluia! Alleluia!* [9]

Notes

[1] KJV.

[2] Charles Gore (1853-1932), Bishop of Oxford, scholar and influential Anglo-Catholic writer.

[3] 2 Corinthians 4:18.

[4] Acts 7:56 (KJV).

[5] cf. Hebrews 11:24-25.

[6] John 14:30.

[7] cf. John 16:33.

[8] Revelation 12:11.

[9] From the hymn 'For all the saints', by Bishop William Walsham How (1864).

Ascensiontide

All authority has been given me in heaven and on earth. Go therefore and make disciples of all the nations ... and lo, I am with you always, even to the end of the age.

Matthew 28:18-20

None of us likes farewells. 'Goodbye' is a word we find difficult to say. Ascension Day this week brings us to a farewell that turns out, after all, not to be a farewell at all. It ends in joyous laughter instead of tears. Why?

JESUS MADE THE GREATEST CLAIM OF HISTORY

"All authority has been given me in heaven and on earth." The strength and conviction of authority is what we need in the present day, especially when so many voices claim authority. In the midst of this clash and din of men's conflicting ideas about God, we need a final source of authority stronger than theirs. It is the authority of a king or president at the back of a nation which gives it the power of unity and its power to wield its sword. The strength of a nation weakens immediately its authority is undermined. In fact, human authorities are often undermined.

Ascensiontide points us to the One whose supreme authority can never be undermined or altered. "All authority has been given me." It was with those words Jesus Christ ascended the throne of God eternal in the heavens. He made the incomparable claim of unlimited authority, not only on earth but in heaven. His authority swept the furthest reaches of heaven and earth over all realms, mortal, material and moral. He had proved it over and over again. Over the realm of creation, the realm of nature: "Even the winds and waves obey him."[1] In the realm of morals, we are told, "No man forgives sins but God."[2] "No man ever spoke like this man."[3] For a while the Cross made the disciples falter; now on the resurrection side of the grave they had proved his authority over life and death.

In Ephesians 1:21 Paul tells us that Christ is on the throne "far above all principality, and power, and might, and dominion, and every name that is named, not only in this world, but also in that which is to come."[4] The things of material force and greed may seem to dominate for a time, but God's dominion is above theirs. "They shall perish but you will remain."[5] We say: "For thine is the kingdom, the power and the glory for ever and ever." Do we believe it? Then we shouldn't be despondent.

THE COMPULSION OF HIS AUTHORITY

"Go therefore..." Because you are fit to be missionaries? To call people to discipleship? No. It is because of Jesus' power and authority to send us. He looked into the faces of men who only had the authority of fishermen and tax-gatherers, and said, "Go on my mission. My authority is behind you. Go on my authority. Not only do you go on my authority but my authority goes with you."

THE CONTINUANCE OF HIS AUTHORITY

"Lo, I am with you always even to the end of the age," even to the utmost limit of time. If we have felt that the power and authority of the ascended Christ has removed him far beyond our reach, we are wrong. His gracious power reaches right down to you and me just where we are with our problems. "Lo, I am with you" – to lift you, not to leave you.

Jesus says to us, "I know you dread many things – that worry tries to dominate you – but I am still the Supreme Power. I am with you to give you the power of ascension above everyone else's domination and above your self." Do you sometimes feel earthbound? Not only the souls of those who cannot leave this earth when their bodies leave it, are earthbound. Jesus is with us to show us a way of escape on to a higher level. The way of ascension is from self to him, from jealousy to love, from despair to hope, from temporal to eternal things. Above the clouds, it's clear blue.

"Lo, I am with you..." He did not say, "Wait until you have built a cathedral or a church, and I will be there." No, "I will be with you wherever you are, in sickness and in health, in joy and in sorrow."

The greatest claim – the greatest compulsion – the furthest continuance of his authority.

Give him the realm of your own life.

Notes

[1]   cf. Matthew 8:27.
[2]   cf. Mark 2:7.
[3]   John 7:46.
[4]   KJV.

Notes Continued

[5] cf. Hebrews 1:11.

Looks

Jesus, looking at him, loved him.

Mark 10:21

How much meaning there is in a look! A strong look is very much more expressive than words. We say, "If looks could kill!" Some people reserve that look for when another car driver nearly involves them in an accident! There is a cold and withering look. There is a look of anger or scorn. Many strong men can be silenced by a look.

But there is also an understanding look. If you have been unhappy or depressed or ill and then someone gave you an understanding, sympathetic look, how it heartened you! How many are strengthened by a look of love. My little daughter, Mary, said to me, "Mummy, I can see myself in your eyes." There is truth in that. Those you love are held in the look of your eyes. "Keep me as the apple of your eye. Hide me under the shadow of your wings."[1] That was David's prayer.

Men found themselves in the *look of Jesus:* "Jesus, looking at him, loved him."[2] In that look, Jesus poured out tenderness and love upon the rich young ruler. It was a look that saw beneath the surface. He saw the young man's zeal in the assurance he gave Jesus that he had kept the commandments from his youth up. But Jesus' look was compelling too, and it left no doubt in the young man's mind as to what he was to do to follow Jesus. The look of Jesus penetrated his heart to his real hindrance – his possessions. They were not harmful in themselves, but because they came between him and God, they were dangerous, and Jesus said they must go. The young man did not possess his possessions; they possessed him. The material values made a stronger appeal to him than the spiritual values Jesus had to offer him. Material things have much too strong a hold on us in a materialistic age. If we choose material securities for ourselves and our children, we shall turn away from the look of Jesus very sorrowfully.

We read of the look of Jesus falling on another – Peter. "The Lord turned and looked upon Peter."[3] Peter had been a close follower until the moment of danger, but he had been overconfident. He had been quite sure that whatever the test, his faith in Jesus would never fail. "Lord, I am ready to go with you, both to prison and to death," he had said[4] – and yet he failed. Why? There were four reasons:

1) *He was too sure of himself* – overconfident.
2) *He was unprepared* for the strength of Satan's attack, perhaps by lack of prayer. He didn't feel his need for it.[5] In contrast, Christ's whole preparation for the Cross was prayer.[6]
3) *He followed afar off.*[7] His enthusiasm was on the wane. He lagged behind and allowed other people to get between him and his Lord.
4) *He associated with the enemies of Jesus.* He stood with them and warmed himself at their fire[8] and so he failed his Lord.

"The Lord turned and looked upon Peter." It was that look of deepest love, yet also of pain, disappointment and wounded trust, that broke Peter's heart and made him see where he had gone wrong. He saw that the past opportunities of standing with his Lord were irretrievable, but it was that wounded look of Jesus that brought Peter to repentance and made a new man of him. And that is what happens. Godly sorrow produces repentance.[9] It is not a selfish sorrow, but sorrow for failing and wounding Christ.

What does the look of Jesus hold for me? It brings me the wonderful knowledge that his eyes, so full of love, are upon me. I can say, "You, Lord, see me," even in my humble home. I am not lost, and nothing that I do is hidden from him.

There are ways of avoiding a look; we can avert our eyes and look down. We must meet his look, bring ourselves to meet the penetration of his eyes so that we may be changed by his look, like Peter. Yes, we have denied him every time we have not confessed him by our lives.

We must give him, not just a casual glance, but a steady look. This means lifting up our eyes to meet his, and not focusing them so much upon the ground and the precipice. We should be "looking unto Jesus, the author and finisher of our faith."[10]

Notes

[1] Psalm 17:8.
[2] Mark 10:21. In Luke's account of this story this man is said to be a ruler – Luke 18:18.
[3] Luke 22:61 (KJV).
[4] Luke 22:33.
[5] cf. Luke 22:31-32.
[6] John 17 and Mark 14:32-42 (and parallel accounts in Matthew and Luke).
[7] Mark 14:54a.
[8] Mark 14:54b.

Notes Continued

[9] 2 Corinthians 7:10.

[10] Hebrews 12:2.

Home as a Sanctuary

We all of us have one great thing in common, and that is we are all homemakers. First a house has to be built from a plan, the materials agreed and the foundations laid. There will often be alterations and additions. Then a home has to be made. We never find a home ready-made for us. They don't just happen, and making them means expenditure, not of money, but of heart and mind and will. A home is made by the quality of life lived in it. An empty house is a desolate place. It is not a home. It may be well-built and furnished but it is empty. We've all come across empty houses. They are empty of love and faithfulness, empty of kindness and happiness. They have no soul-life.

The home takes on the personality of the life lived in it. You meet the life of the house as soon as you enter – we call it 'atmosphere' and people make it. It is harmonious or otherwise. If we live alone, it will be made by us. If God lives there it will be made by him. Mary Sumner[1] had a vision of homes made by God. If the life of our homes is made by God, they become 'sanctuaries'. Is that an impossibility?

We are given the meaning of that word in the Bible. The Sanctuary was the Inner Place, the Holy of Holies in the Tabernacle. It was the place where the presence of God dwelt.[2] If our homes are to become sanctuaries, God must dwell in them. We are told so often in the Gospels of the difference made to homes when Christ entered them. Think of the homes of Martha and Mary,[3] of Simon[4] and Matthew.[5] Jesus never forces an entrance into our homes. Do you remember the couple on the Emmaus road? Jesus did not force an entrance; he made as though he would go further, but they constrained him that he would enter and abide with them. When he entered their home, he blessed it and their eyes were opened.[6] He became the life of the home and changed its atmosphere.

Jesus is passing by the homes of England and only those who ask him to enter their homes and lives will be real homemakers and will have open eyes, wide awake to spiritual truths. A prison will be turned into a sanctuary. He shares our common experiences. He shared an ordinary meal and he blessed it. That's what he can do now.

The sanctuary is a place of protection and defence and refuge. Home is the place where a mother first protects her young. God uses her in the defence and training of her baby. What a wonderful responsibility! We cannot fully protect them ourselves without God's help and guidance.

The only way to protect them is to bring them to Jesus that they may "grow in wisdom and in stature and in favour with God and man".[7] Spiritual growth towards the life of God in our home is growth towards the light, the perfect growth. Teach your children to pray by praying yourself; it will then be quite natural to them. Pray with them over difficulties. Include them and let them see you praying.[8] Let God make our homes a place of protection and defence for our children, and later a place of wise sympathy, a refuge for the lonely and homeless these days.

The sanctuary is a holy place. It is made holy by the presence of love. Love sanctifies and "love never fails".[9] Love gets over any obstacles. Love protects the sanctity of marriage. A loving atmosphere is a holy atmosphere because "love does not seek its own".[10] It is a love that gives and gives and does not count the cost. It does not grasp but gives. The love of Jesus lifts the focus of love from ourselves to others.

A sanctuary is a place where an offering is made, a sacrifice. Jesus sacrificed his life. At the heart of our spiritual life stands his Cross. In response, we must make ourselves a constant offering to him in our homes. At the heart of all love is sacrifice. It is an offering not only of ourselves but of those we love. Surrender them. Make them an offering. Don't worry about them. Don't hinder them. Be like Hannah[11] and Abraham.[12] Often they are given back when God sees we are really willing to make them an offering.

A professor once said to a young Christian, "I would give everything in life to possess what you possess." The student replied, "Then you *will* possess it because that is what it cost me – everything – all my life became an offering." May Christ make our lives a sanctuary of his presence.

Notes

[1] Mary Sumner (1828-1921) founded the Mothers' Union in 1876 to support mothers as they brought up their children as Christians. It is now a worldwide movement of over four million members in 84 countries. Our mother became leader of the Street MU branch in 1942.

[2] Exodus 25:22.

[3] Luke 10:38-42.

[4] Mark 1:29-31.

[5] Matthew 9:9-13.

[6] Luke 24:28-31.

[7] cf. Luke 2:52.

Notes Continued

[8] Point 7 of the original Mothers' Union membership card was: "To teach them (my children) to pray daily, and to pray with them." Cordelia Moyse, *A History of the Mothers' Union: Women, Anglicanism and Globalisation 1876-2008* (Boydell Press, 2009), Appendix One.

[9] 1 Corinthians 13:8.

[10] 1 Corinthians 13:5.

[11] 1 Samuel 1:28.

[12] Genesis 22.

The Spiritual Training of Children[1]

Jesus took a child

Mark 9:36

The most obvious thing about our children is that they grow. The most pitiful sight is that of a child stunted in growth, arrested in development. As parents, we all want our children to have a normal, healthy childhood. That means normal development and growth, physical, mental and spiritual.

None of us can tell what that growth will become. What possibilities there are in a child! They are bundles of undeveloped possibilities. First, it is essential to recognise the wonderful qualities in a child. Learn from them; respect them. Our Lord Jesus found in a child all the qualifications necessary for entrance into the kingdom of heaven. He listened patiently to his disciples wrangling for position and power in the kingdom but, in the end, he took a child and set him in the midst.[2] A child was given first place! He was the centre of attention that day for, as Jesus had said, "of such is the kingdom of heaven".[3]

Our children are the hope of the future. A Christian England depends on them. We show our concern for them in our care of their bodies and minds – in their physical and intellectual growth. We often fail to care for the most important part of them, the only lasting part – their immortal souls. Because of this, their growth is stunted, they are spiritual dwarfs. A great deal is being done to preserve Religious Education in our day schools and Sunday Schools but, if that teaching is not also carried out at home, the children won't be convinced by it. The most powerful influence in a child's life is and will always be the *home influence*. The roots of childhood are grown in the soil of home life. On the depth and strength of those roots depends the whole growth of the child. The firmest roots are grown in the first seven years, when a child is most impressionable and sensitive to atmosphere. What you mould in wax, you cast in stone.[4]

Jesus took a child. Let his influence shape your children. The mothers, we read, "brought their children to Jesus".[5] They are too much of a responsibility for us alone. How often we read in history and in the Bible of the life of a wonderful man or woman who was dedicated to God in childhood by his or her parents![6] This dedication comes through the dedication of the *parents* to God. In baptism we bring our children and Jesus takes them. First of all *we* give them, and then later *they* give themselves.[7] Many of our famous men and women have become famous because our Lord took them as children, when they were most open to the influences of God. Are we doing all we can for their spiritual growth by bringing them to Jesus, and letting him take them? Don't stand in their way; let them come to him. Don't shut them out of their spiritual privileges, including the Eucharist.

The growth of the soul depends upon faith. Faith is natural to a child.[8] We see their implicit faith in us and in God. The unseen is so natural to them. They are not earthbound; their world is peopled with invisible beings. The fact that God is unseen does not worry them. They are capable of much greater faith than we ourselves.

Prayer is as natural as breathing to a child. If we fail to teach them to pray, we stifle their souls' growth. We teach them to talk from the first; we must teach their souls to talk in prayer to God. But we cannot do this unless we ourselves can pray. Also read the Bible to them. One child said, "I think the Bible is more exciting than any of my books." Make it live in their minds – the parables are particularly likely to fire their imaginations.

Jesus took a child. Let him take yours to bless and use them as he will. He is our childhood's pattern; day by day like us he grew.[9] He alone has brought spiritual growth to perfection, as we see from his own perfect childhood: "He grew in wisdom and in stature and in favour with God and man."[10] He grew towards God. All growth must be towards the light; don't let us come between our children and the light of God.

Notes

[1] Like the previous talk, this talk reveals the influence of the teaching of the Mothers' Union, and was surely delivered after Mother became Mothers' Union Enrolling Member in Street in 1942.

[2] Mark 9:33-37.

[3] Matthew 19:14, cf. Mark 10:14.

[4] "Every one who knew Mrs. Sumner (founder of Mothers' Union) will recall her insistence upon the 'first ten years' as the especial portion of a mother in her child's life, the period in which she can exercise her great prerogative of moulding its character into a form that shall survive through all succeeding influences." Before the end of her life she became convinced it was the first *seven* years. Horatia Erskine, *Mary Sumner, Her Life and Work* (Warren & Son, 1921), pp. 26, 88.

[5] cf. Mark 10:13.

Notes Continued

6 An obvious example in the Bible is Samuel, dedicated to God by his mother Hannah (1 Samuel 1:28). Among other children so dedicated in history were St. Gregory of Nazianzus (4th century) and evidently John and Charles Wesley (18th century).

7 That is the purpose of Confirmation, though their personal commitment to Christ can come at any time.

8 Mary Sumner said, "The gradual unfolding of a child's mind is profoundly interesting; you have to secure his heart and his imagination ... Little children are born with a religious instinct; they value sympathy, and the tender love and protecting care of the Lord Jesus brings joy into their lives, and allays sorrow and fear. A boy of four years old told me that when he was frightened in the dark, he asked our Lord to come close to him, and take care of him, 'and then,' said he, 'I wasn't afraid any more.'" *Mary Sumner* by Horatia Erskine, p.15.

9 Echoing words from the hymn 'Once in royal David's city', by Cecil Frances Alexander (1848).

10 cf. Luke 2:52.

A Charge to Combined Parochial Church Councils

I speak this afternoon as myself a member of a PCC[1] and I am putting myself under examination. As the Diocesan Mission has progressed, we have begun to feel that in the past we have missed many opportunities of witnessing to our Lord. One of our opportunities has been in our PCC Meetings. For years we have sat round the parish hall, secretly if not apparently very bored, and only lending half an ear to the proceedings! I think we have often felt it to be a waste of our time, but we have only just realised what a waste it has been of God's time – the time he has given us in which to serve him.

There is a prayer which we need to pray and act upon: "Thou who hast called us to thy service, make us worthy of thy calling." The members of the Early Church were worthy of their calling. We read that as a result of their first Church Council Meeting 3,000 souls were added to the Church.[2] The deepest need in the heart of humanity is a spiritual need. For those of us who seek to serve our Lord, the spiritual realm must have first claim. We are not to be so concerned over material things – they are a necessary concern but not our chief one. Our focus should not be merely the addition of beautiful church furnishings but of the souls of men and women to the church.

HOW IS OUR SERVICE TO BE MADE EFFECTIVE?

1) The first need of the Early Church was for members to witness to an experience of the living Christ. On their convincing evidence of his resurrection and of his living presence within them hung the future of the Church. Many people live today as if Christ were not a living reality – as if he had never risen from the dead. It still remains the greatest need of the Church to give the world convincing evidence of our Lord's living, vital presence.

2) We must have first-hand knowledge of his presence in our own lives before we can convince anyone else. The evidence the disciples gave was so strong because they spoke from first-hand knowledge of his risen presence. They said, "That which we have heard, which we have seen, and have looked upon, and have handled, of the Word of Life, we declare to you."[3] They were

convincing in their enthusiasm. Enthusiasm kindles enthusiasm. I wonder how convincing we are in this way? The prospect of a PCC Meeting doesn't usually arouse much enthusiasm! It was different when St. Peter and St. John and St. Paul called their Church Council Meetings. How fiercely the fire of enthusiasm burned in their midst – a fire that welded them together, until there was an affinity of purpose and they were of one mind and soul, kindled by one flame! There was no lukewarmness about them!

We so often stand condemned with the Church of Laodicea for our tepid faith.[4] A wavering, fluctuating faith is so utterly unconvincing. The indifference outside the Church springs from one source – the tepid witness from those within. The greatest harm done to Christianity is done by the Christians. Those in the Early Church gave convincing evidence through their prayer life. All their preparation for their service to our Lord was made with prayer. When they prayed the place was shaken, the strongholds of Satan were shaken, and the people were shaken and the Holy Spirit came upon them.[5]

The vision of our Lord for his Church was this: "My Father's house shall be called a house of prayer."[6] A house of prayer can only be made by praying men and women. The responsibility is ours – not only the Parson's! As the inner circle of the Church, we must prepare for each Sunday by prayer and, if we are critical of our Parson, we must pray for him.

3) For those of us who feel we have failed to be worthy of his service, our Lord never fails to give us fresh opportunities. To St. Peter who had publicly denied him thrice, he gave the opportunity of acknowledging him thrice.[7] When we ourselves meet him on the shore of our lives, he rekindles a fire of love in our hearts.[8] We find then that love is the only motive he wants in our service. It is not more knowledge we need but more love. We who have had much to do with church affairs have not always known the emphasis to be placed there. Jesus asks us, "Do you love me?" He uses the Greek word *agapas* which is different from *phileō*, the one used by St. Peter in his reply. Jesus was asking, "Do you love me *devotedly*, not just emotionally?" – with a burning flame that consumes all lesser loves.

I came across this prayer recently for deliverance "from the insincerity that says, 'Lord, you know that I love you,' yet refuses to feed his sheep." That is the test of our love for him. In so far as our devotion is given to him, our service will be given to others. The love of Christ constrains us.[9] To love our Lord means to identify ourselves with his cares, his sheep. By love we must serve one another. The badge of his service is humility and the emblems of that service are a towel and a basin.[10]

Notes

[1] Street Parochial Church Council minutes reveal mother was appointed a PCC member in June 1940. At the Annual Parochial Church Meeting in April 1941 she was chosen as one of the parish's "Ruri-Decanal representatives". Perhaps it was in that capacity that she subsequently gave this talk at a Ruri-Decanal Conference (equivalent to our Deanery Synod). The evangelistic tone of the talk suggests it was actually intended as part of the Diocesan Mission.

[2] cf. Acts 2:41.

[3] cf. 1 John 1:1, 3.

[4] Revelation 3:15-16.

[5] Acts 4:31.

[6] cf. Mark 11:17, Isaiah 56:7.

[7] John 18:25-27, 21:15-17.

[8] cf. John 21:9.

[9] 2 Corinthians 5:14.

[10] John 13:4-5.

The Peace of God

You will keep him in perfect peace, whose mind is stayed on You.

Isaiah 26:3

Ten months ago we were hunting out our old flags to hang from our windows on the Declaration of Peace.[1] Our hearts were filled with a wild joy and a great sense of relief, though the relief was tempered with anguish of heart over the loss and suffering caused by war. "Grant us peace in our time, O Lord" had been our fervent prayer for years. Yet we find that peace does not come easily or suddenly with the firing of the last shot. We find that much of our so-called peace has been shattered by the threat of further inevitable disasters and impending doom and destruction. We are only too conscious of a deep distrust between nations, an air of unrest and uncertainty. There is a desolate cry of "Peace, peace, where there is no peace".[2]

Why does peace seem to evade us? Is it that we have sought it from the wrong source? A traveller came to a stream and as he bent down to drink the water, a man saw him and ran to him and begged him not to drink. "That water is polluted," he said. "Get back to the source. The stream collects mud and refuse as it progresses." The stream of our lives is also often polluted by man's systems, plans and conferences. We must get back to the source. The source of our peace is God.

Peace comes from God, not through any human agency. It is "the peace of God which passes all human understanding that shall keep our hearts".[3] In God, our hearts are at the source of every precious thing.[4] Some of us have been impressed by the answers of the Brains' Trust panel on the wireless to the question, "Is there any hope of permanent peace?" The answer given by Lord Elton and others was, "Only through a change of heart or a spiritual conversion." It is the first duty of the Church to strive for worldwide conversions. Without Christ, we cannot have peace in our hearts or peace in the world, and any amount of false unity without God will not bring peace.

Jesus wept over the city of Jerusalem just before they crucified him and cried out, "If you had known ... the things that make for your peace!"[5] When they rejected him, they rejected all things that belonged to their peace. Whenever he is rejected there will be no peace. He looks out now over the vast areas of our cities that are rejecting him, casting him out, crucifying him, and laments afresh, "If you had known...!" We reject him when we reject his commands. "Peace be with you,"[6] was always his way of approach to the human soul. We need his peace of reconciliation between God and ourselves, the peace of his forgiveness and reconciliation with each other, and between nations.

Our Lord had nothing materially to leave his disciples but he had something far greater to leave them – the legacy of peace: "My peace I give to you; not as the world gives do I give to you."[7] He spoke of "my peace" – not from struggle and persecution and suffering – but his unbroken peace in the midst of it all. His peace was the peace that he possessed through his fiery trial, the peace which laid a cool hand on his lips so that that he "answered them nothing".[8] Earlier on, his serenity had enabled him to sleep at the height of the storm.[9] His peace came through surrender to his Father's will, the peace he gives to all who love and trust him.

I am reminded of the dramatic scene in the play *Thomas à Becket*. The atmosphere was charged with evil temptations, intrigue and treachery which eventually led to Thomas's murder. The scene shows him standing in the pulpit of Canterbury Cathedral for his last sermon. He was a calm and dignified figure and his text was, "My peace I give unto you." Yes, he had in his quiet hands the possession of peace.

What are the conditions for receiving the peace of God? In the words of our text, "You will keep him in perfect peace, whose mind is stayed on You." These are Christ's peace terms – the unconditional surrender of our lives to him. We have come today to stay our minds on him in prayer, to centre our minds on him. Peace is never given to those who centre their minds on themselves. It has been said, "Find out the centre of a man's thoughts and you will find his god." At the heart of every cyclone there is a place of absolute stillness, where a leaf will not stir, where a baby may sleep undisturbed. For those who centre their hearts and minds on Jesus lies this truth: at the heart of every danger, every bereavement, every anxiety our Saviour can be to us that quiet place of refuge where his peace will keep our hearts and minds in the knowledge and love of God.[10]

> *Drop thy still dews of quietness,*
> *Till all our strivings cease;*
> *Take from our souls the strain and stress,*
> *And let our ordered lives confess*

The beauty of thy peace.[11]

Notes

1. The German unconditional surrender on May 8, 1945 – V.E. Day.
2. cf. Jeremiah 6:14.
3. cf. Philippians 4:7.
4. cf. James 1:17.
5. Luke 19:42.
6. John 20:19, 26, cf. Luke 24:36. This was the normal Jewish greeting.
7. John 14:27.
8. cf. Mark 14:61, 15:3, 5.
9. Mark 4:37-38.
10. cf. John 14:27.
11. From the hymn 'Dear Lord and Father of mankind', by John Greenleaf Whittier (1872).

Gravesend and Hove

Friendship[1]

Henceforth I call you not servants but friends.

John 15:15 (KJV)

One of the dreads of childhood is being alone. That dread attacks old and young alike.

THE NEED OF FRIENDSHIP

We need friendship because God has not made us to live alone. There is no such thing as a solitary Christian. The Church is a Christian fellowship or family. There is no time in our lives when we are totally independent of each other, not in childhood, nor in marriage, nor in old age. The hunger of the human heart is for friendship, to share our life with another. We need someone who understands us, to whom we can tell our secrets, our longings and joys and troubles.

This great Girls' Friendly Society (GFS) to which you belong recognises this fact that we all have a need for friendship.

THE INFLUENCE UPON US OF OUR FRIENDS

How greatly influenced we all have been, and are, by our friends! We may never know to what extent. Here in your branch you have a great opportunity to make friends who will be a help to you.

Bad friends can drag us down and lead us away from all that we know to be good. If you have formed a harmful friendship, *break it*. Jesus said, "If your right hand causes you to sin, cut it off."[2] Make a clean break.

THE BEST FRIENDSHIP

The GFS exists to help us form the best friendship of all – friendship with God. Jesus said, "Henceforth I call you not servants but friends."[3] We are invited right into that close friendship with God. It used to be a comfort to me when I was a child, and feeling lonely, to sing the chorus 'There's a friend for little children'[4] – only, I have since learned that he is not "above the clear blue sky" but close to me. Jesus said to his disciples, "Lo, I am with you always, even unto the end of the world."[5]

Abraham was called "the friend of God". He lived so close to God that he experienced this most wonderful of all friendships. There are many who know *about* God but not very many who *know* God. Jesus said, "This is life eternal, to know God."[6]

At a concert one night, a famous singer sang Psalm 23 faultlessly. When he had finished the psalm, an old and frail clergyman rose from his seat and asked if he might be allowed to sing the same psalm. He sang it with deep feeling and devotion. At the end the singer came up to him and said quite simply, "I know the psalm, *you* know the Shepherd." To know God is quite different from knowing about him.

THE FRIEND OF SINNERS

Abraham was a man of great faith and obedience. Of course, *he* could be called "the friend of God", but I am so unworthy. It seems impossible for me. And yet Jesus was called "the friend of sinners". He comes right down beside us, a friend who never fails, whose love can never die. His love for us has stood the greatest test. He said, "Greater love has no one than this, than to lay down one's life for his friends."[7]

Notes

[1] This talk must have been given in 1948 as parish magazines show St. Mary's church had a branch of the GFS then, which was superseded by a new branch of the AYPA (Anglican Young People's Association) early in 1949.

[2] Matthew 5:30.

[3] John 15:15 (KJV).

[4] By Albert Midlane (1859).

[5] cf. Matthew 28:20.

[6] cf. John 17:3.

[7] John 15:13.

The Value of the Old Testament

God, who at various times and in various ways spoke in time past to the fathers by the prophets, has in these last days spoken to us by his Son.

Hebrews 1:1-2

Here is a summary of both the Old Testament and the New Testament:

The Bible is unique. There is no book to equal it in human literature for it contains the purest moral teaching, the sublimest poetry, the noblest sentiments, the clearest information about both the origin and the end of all things. It is not one book but a library of books, 66 in all, written by at least 40 different people and in three different languages.[1]

The Pentateuch (or first five books of the Bible), the Psalms and books of some of the prophets were in existence in our Lord's day and were his Bible,[2] and were quoted by him. For example, in Luke 4:17-19 he quoted from Isaiah 61:1-2. The three different languages in which we know that different books were written were Hebrew, Greek and Aramaic. The Old Testament has been said to record man's search for God, and the New Testament, God's search for man. Through both of them is revealed the character of God, the nature of sin and our need of redemption.

Through the Old Testament, we see God's great desire to speak and make contact with mankind. He was always endeavouring to convey his thought to his people. He took the instrument of his chosen race, Israel, and he worked through that nation in the world. He revealed to the chosen race the truth that in the beginning, he had created the world, and that at the height of his creation was man. He saw that everything he created was good. Through man's disobedience came sin and the need for repentance and forgiveness.

God raised up leaders, the great Fathers or Patriarchs, Abraham, Isaac, Jacob and Joseph. Moses, whose face shone from meeting with God,[3] instilled into the people of Israel God's thoughts, his commandments, his moral laws. He promised to make his chosen race a great nation and to give them possession of Canaan, a land flowing with milk and honey where the peoples of the world would find blessing. God ruled Israel through leaders: judges, kings and priests, and by his revealed law and his royal heralds and prophets – "God who at various times and in various ways spoke in times past to the fathers *by the prophets.*"

The prophets constantly recalled his people, warning them of personal and national disaster if they persisted in their sinful ways. They learned of the holiness of God and the need for an offering for sin. Always they looked forward to the coming of a Messiah, a Saviour. The Passover Lamb prepared them for "the Lamb of God who takes away the sin of the world".[4]

The word 'testament' means 'covenant', promises made between God and his children. Though the differences between the Old and New Testaments are radical and vital, these Covenants are not opposed to each other. In the Old we have the symbol, but in the New we have the substance. In the Old we have the water, but in the New we have the wine. Let us avoid thinking that now we have the New Covenant the Old has no message for us. On the contrary, there is nothing in the New Testament that is not forecast in the Old. "For the New is in the Old contained, the Old is in the New explained."[5] "God, who ... spoke in times past to the fathers by the prophets ... has in these last days spoken to us *by his Son.*"

All this time God had been trying to convey his thought to man. Thought cannot be conveyed except by words. We may all wish to convey our thoughts to each other at this moment, but we cannot do so unless we express them in words. "In the beginning was the Word, and the Word was with God and the Word was God ... And the Word was made flesh and dwelt among us and we beheld his glory, the glory as of the only begotten of the Father."[6] He is the language of God interpreting God's thoughts to us.

Jesus said to his two disciples on the Emmaus road who failed to recognise him after the crucifixion, "O foolish ones, and slow of heart to believe in all that the prophets have spoken ... And beginning at Moses and all the prophets, he expounded to them in all the Scriptures the things concerning himself." And later we read again, "He opened their understanding that they might comprehend the Scriptures."[7]

Let us close with the Scripture Union motto or prayer, "Open my eyes, that I may see wondrous things from your law."[8]

Notes

1   The source of this quotation has not been traced but perhaps it is from one of the books of the Rev. Dr. W. Graham Scroggie, who was a visiting lecturer and sometime Vice-President of Ridgelands Bible College.

2   cf. Luke 24:44.

3   Exodus 34:29-35.

4   John 1:29

5   In his book *Fascination of the Old Testament Story* (London: Marshall, Morgan & Scott, 1930) p.13, W. G. Scroggie introduces this statement with the words, "as has been tersely said…"

6   John 1:1, 14 (KJV).

7   Luke 24:25, 27, 45.

8   Psalm 119:18.

The Work of the Holy Spirit

Nevertheless I tell you the truth. It is to your advantage that I go away; for if I do not go away, the Helper will not come to you; but if I depart, I will send Him to you. And when He has come, He will convict the world of sin, and of righteousness, and of judgment: of sin, because they do not believe in Me; of righteousness, because I go to My Father and you see Me no more; of judgment, because the ruler of this world is judged. "I still have many things to say to you, but you cannot bear them now. However, when He, the Spirit of truth, has come, He will guide you into all truth; for He will not speak on His own authority, but whatever He hears He will speak; and He will tell you things to come. He will glorify Me, for He will take of what is Mine and declare it to you.

John 16:7-14

The Holy Spirit does three things: he brings a conviction of sin, he guides us into all truth, and he glorifies our Lord Jesus Christ.

THE HOLY SPIRIT BRINGS A CONVICTION OF SIN

A clergyman attending a meeting of psychiatrists said later, "They have invented an 11th Commandment: 'Thou shalt have no guilt'!" The sun shines into our rooms and shows up the dirt. Our Lord Jesus shines into our hearts and reveals sin. He turns out the rubbish, all that is worthless, and he refurnishes the room of our hearts. At the beginning of our Communion service we pray, "Oh God, unto whom all hearts are open, all desires are known and from whom our secrets are not hid, cleanse the thoughts of our hearts by the inspiration of thy Holy Spirit..."[1]

Instead of finding fault in each other, we must find fault *in ourselves*. Hold on to what is good in others and pray for them. You can't be angry and pray for someone at the same time. Pray for the evangelists who are being used by the Holy Spirit to reprove and convict the world of sin. We must forsake before we can follow.

THE HOLY SPIRIT IS TO BE OUR GUIDE

So often we want 'to lead our own lives'. If the Holy Spirit is to guide us, we must be led by him. "As many as are led by the Spirit of God, they are the sons of God."[2] The early disciples were led by the Holy Spirit in every detail of their lives. The Acts of the Apostles might well be called 'The Acts of the Holy Spirit'. The apostles never planned their work without waiting upon God in prayer and putting themselves at the disposal of the Holy Spirit. We should pray, "Into your hands I commend my spirit"[3] at the beginning of our day as well as at the end. The apostles were so absolutely obedient to the compulsions of the Holy Spirit.

When people and their needs are laid on our hearts, it may be that we should visit them. We are told, "Do not quench the Spirit,"[4] and, "Do not grieve the Holy Spirit."[5] We must be obedient and ready to be used by God.

THE HOLY SPIRIT GLORIFIES OUR LORD JESUS IN OUR LIVES

Test a movement in our heart by asking, "How much glory does this bring to my Lord and Saviour?" Or by saying, "He must increase but I must decrease,"[6] or, "My soul magnifies the Lord."[7] When there is a harvest of the fruit of the Holy Spirit in our lives, we glorify Jesus. The fruit are love, joy, peace, patience, gentleness, goodness, faith, humility and self-control.[8] Jesus said, "If you … being evil, know how to give good gifts to your children, how much more will your heavenly Father give the Holy Spirit to those who ask him."[9]

Notes

[1] *The Book of Common Prayer* (1662) Holy Communion service, with slight variations.
[2] Romans 8:14 (KJV).
[3] cf. Luke 23:46.
[4] 1 Thessalonians 5:19.
[5] Ephesians 4:30.
[6] cf. John 3:30.
[7] Luke 1:46.
[8] Galatians 5:22-23 (KJV). The Greek word *pistis* can be translated both 'faith' and 'faithfulness'.
[9] Luke 11:13.

Christfilter Our Hope[1]

*The God of hope fill you with all joy and peace in believing,
that you may abound in hope, by the power of the Holy Spirit.*

Romans 15:13

How many of us in these days give way to depression? It is easy to darken each other's days! When we cease to hope, we lose our courage and we lose our sense of any purpose in life. Hope is an essential ingredient in the art of living. Hope is like salt in sea water that gives us buoyancy and refuses to let us sink.

In the midst of danger, such as war, we are sustained by the hope of deliverance. In times of hardship, we are sustained by the hope of better times ahead of us. In sickness, we are sustained by the hope of recovery. "While there is life, there is hope," says the doctor, as he seeks to fan the spark of life into a flame. In the darkest night of experience, we are sustained by the hope of the dawn and a new day. This thought came to me so strongly when three of us took a twelve-hour night flight to America. The night seemed endless and yet the dawn *did* come. And in childbirth, the pain gives way to rejoicing when the baby is born.

In the cold and dreariness of winter God implants in our hearts the hope of spring. It is hope that keeps us ever looking forwards and not backwards. The hope in our hearts is the proof of the immortality of our souls. "Hope springs eternal in the human breast"[2] because it springs from the heart of the Eternal. "The God of all hope fill you with joy in believing that you may abound in hope."[3] Our faith is stimulated by hope. In Hebrews 11:1 we read, "Now faith is the substance of *things hoped for*, the evidence of things not seen." Hope carries us far beyond the boundaries and limitations of this world. In our Saviour Jesus Christ, all our hopes are fulfilled. He was the fulfilment of hope in history. Into the hearts of the people of Israel God had implanted the hope of the coming of the Messiah. Every Jewish mother who bore a son hoped he might be the promised Saviour. They looked forward with eager expectancy.

There was an old man of God, just and devout, waiting for the consolation – the hope of Israel. When a lowly mother came and put into his arms her precious babe, the hope of ages was fulfilled and he prayed, "Lord, now you are letting your servant depart in peace ... for my eyes have seen your salvation."[4] The Saviour of the world had come. When we take him as our Saviour, like Simeon, the hope of peace and forgiveness is fulfilled for us.

Jesus Christ is to be the fulfilment of present and future history. In Acts 1:11 we read, "This same Jesus, who was taken up from you into heaven, will so come in like manner as you saw him go into heaven." The land into which Jesus had been born holds the central position geographically in the world. We have this sure and certain hope that he will return in glory to the very centre and heart of this war-torn world, and ultimately, "the government will be upon his shoulder"[5] and "the earth shall be filled with the knowledge of the glory of God as the waters cover the sea".[6]

Christ is our hope of life beyond this world. There was very little in Old Testament Scriptures to teach about life after death. To Israelites it was a shadow existence.[7] In Christ we reach out to boundaries beyond the limitation of our sight. St. Paul rightly declares, "If in this life only we have faith in Christ, we are of all men most miserable."[8] But soon we shall come to Easter when we shall be thinking of "life out of death, the endless mystery". Then our Saviour proved by the power of his resurrection that to "those who trust him wholly, he is wholly true".[9] He said, "I am the resurrection and the life. He who believes in me ... shall never die."[10] We have heard these words recently at the King's funeral.[11] These words bring great comfort to the bereaved.

Are you ever tempted to feel that life is without hope? A Japanese Christian returned to search for his parents in the ruined city of Hiroshima. Before he left, he spent a few minutes in the garden where they had lived. Practically nothing was left, no green leaves anywhere, no birds flying in the air. A mysterious silence prevailed; all around was death and desolation. He asked himself whether the Japanese would ever raise their heads again and strive for reconstruction. "Suddenly," he said, "I found myself gazing at a single spot. At the mangled root of a burned banana tree, a fresh green shoot was peeping. It reminded me of the creative, vital power which had fought the destructive force of the atom bomb for these ten days, and had already broken through the burned earth. It had been working under the ground while we were in despair. I heard the words of Christ, 'If God so clothes the grass of the field ... shall he not much more clothe you, O ye of little faith?'[12] I came to Hiroshima in despair but I left in hope."

Let us "lay hold upon the hope set before us, which hope we have as an anchor of the soul, both sure and steadfast".[13]

Notes

1 A talk delivered in the late winter or early spring of 1952.
2 From *An Essay on Man* (1734), by Alexander Pope.
3 Romans 15:13.
4 Luke 2:29-30.
5 Isaiah 9:6.
6 cf. Habakkuk 2:14.
7 e.g. Psalm 88:4-5.
8 cf. 1 Corinthians 15:19.
9 From the hymn 'Like a river glorious', by Frances Ridley Havergal (1876).
10 John 11:25-26.
11 The funeral of King George VI on February 15, 1952.
12 Matthew 6:30 (KJV).
13 Hebrews 6:18-19 (KJV).

Holy Ground

The place where you stand is holy ground.

Exodus 3:5

On Sunday we had the hallowing of the House of Prayer by the Bishop.[1] A place of prayer is a place which is set apart for God.

As well as that, the place on which *we* stand – our ordinary daily life, must be hallowed and set apart for God. It was while Moses was doing his ordinary, domestic task of minding sheep, that the call of God came to him. It was not in a spectacular place, not merely the desert but the 'backside' of the desert.[2] One might have thought in such a place Moses was lost, hidden from everyone, but he was not hidden from God. Often our lives are lived in some remote backwater and we think that what we are doing is of no value to God. We may think to ourselves, "If only things had been different... I would have done this or I would have done that." But God is with us where we are, wanting to hallow our daily task.

God sets the ordinary bush of the desert on fire with the light of his presence. We know the words of the well-known hymn:

Breathe on me, Breath of God,
Till I am wholly thine,
Until this earthly part of me
Glows with thy fire divine.[3]

To be holy, we must be wholly his. The ordinary things we do in love for each other may also glow with the light of his presence. Make everything an offering to him and it becomes transformed.

Take off your shoes "for the place where you stand is holy ground". We show reverence for God and the things of God when we recognise his presence. Albert Schweitzer said, "It was a reverence for life that made me do my utmost to preserve life in my medical mission."[4] There is so little reverence these days; love and life are sinned against and taken so lightly.

Taking off one's shoes was an Eastern custom, one of removing dust and defilement before entering a house or the Holy of the Holies in the Temple. In Christ's presence there must be for all of us the discarding of sin in our lives.

Breathe on me, Breath of God,
Until my heart is pure.

Small sins, if allowed to remain, can fester and poison the whole of our lives, like a splinter or thorn left in a finger. Sometimes we seek God's blessing and healing and wonder why we don't seem to receive it.

Our little daughter, Ruth, had a very inflamed eye. We gave her eye baths and eye drops and neither did her any good. It was only when we took her to a specialist – who first of all shone his brilliant light into her eye and revealed a speck of rust which was causing all the trouble, then removed the speck and her eye became healthy once more – that she was able to enjoy life again. I thought of the way Christ shines the light of his holiness into our lives and reveals the specks of sin that spoil our lives for us. He reveals to remove. "Be holy, for I am holy."[5]

Take your sandals off your feet, for the place where you stand
is holy ground.

Notes

[1] This surely refers to the dedication of St. George's Church, Gravesend, as the country's first ecumenical Chapel of Unity (a Pocahontas memorial) by the Bishop of Rochester, the Rt. Revd. Christopher Chavasse, on November 1st, 1952. American-born Lady Nancy Astor, first female Member of the British Parliament, referred to it as a "House of Prayer" in the words she spoke at the service. This talk of Mother must have been given in the first week of November 1952, perhaps to the Martha and Mary group in the parish, founded in May 1951, of which she was leader.

[2] Exodus 3:1 (KJV).

[3] By Edwin Hatch (1878).

[4] Dr. Albert Schweitzer opened a hospital in Lambaréné in French Equatorial Africa (later Gabon) in 1913, which he ran until his death in 1965.

[5] Leviticus 11:45.

Women's World Day of Prayer[1]

For the earth shall be filled with the knowledge of the glory of the Lord, as the waters cover the sea.

Habakkuk 2:14

Today we are bidden 'to go forward'. We must have a goal in view and it must be nothing less than that the whole world is filled with the glory of God. We do not want war – but love. Love spans the world. It is the universal language understood by all races including South Africa, Russia and Japan. The magnet of God's love draws all men. Jesus said, "I, if I be lifted up ... will draw all men unto me."[2]

How can we achieve this object? First, by *united effort*. There is strength in unity. On this great day we are helping to answer our Lord's prayer "that they may be one as we are one".[3] We must close our ranks against the rising tide of Communism. We have made great strides forward in uniting. We have powerful examples in the life of Bishop Bell,[4] in the countries of Europe since the war,[5] and in the World Council of Churches. World conferences of that Council have been held in Evanston[6] and in Holland.[7] The meeting point between the churches is the recognition of the divinity of Christ. There has been also the formation of the Church of South India.[8] In England, there has been an interchange of pulpits between different denominations. What was it that brought about such a great work of the Holy Spirit?

It was *prayer*. "More things are wrought by prayer than this world dreams of."[9] I am proud to think it was the *women* of the world who took the initiative in bringing this, the greatest unifying power in the world, to bear on world problems. Today a great volume of prayer goes up from 145 countries. It is prayer day and night – as those in one country finish, we begin! In Blackpool, there was darkness over the whole city until the Mayor touched the master switch and every light blazed.[10] Today we touch the master switch of prayer and light goes on over all the world provided that every light bulb is connected to the mains.

- Someone lonely, far from civilisation, suddenly feels conscious of the presence of Jesus – because of our prayers.
- Someone in moral or physical danger is strengthened to resist temptation and is guided into safety – because of our prayers.

- Someone who has been drawn right away from God by worldly pleasures, suddenly feels the emptiness of life without God: "And from the best bliss the world imparts, they turn unfilled to thee again"[11] – because of our prayers.

Our Lord is the greatest intercessor and we unite with him. He prays for us today as he did for the first disciples, "Holy Father, keep through your name those whom you have given me ... I do not pray that you should take them out of the world, but that you should keep them from the evil one."[12] Through our lives and through our prayers may we be made his instruments. What a wonderful thing if the outcome of today could be that we each pledge ourselves to give an extra ten minutes a day in prayer for the world!

O Lord make me an instrument of thy peace,
Where there is hatred let me put love,
Where there is resentment, let me put forgiveness,
Where there is discord, let me put unity,
Where there is doubt, let me put faith,
Where there is despair, let me bring happiness,
Where there is sadness, let me bring joy,
Where there is darkness, let me bring light.[13]

Notes

[1] A talk to an ecumenical group of women in Hove, it seems, on the Women's World Day of Prayer, the first Friday in March in 1958 or possibly a year or two earlier. This special day was started in the USA in 1887 and came to the British Isles in the 1930s. It is ecumenical and brings together women of different races, cultures and traditions. (Wikipedia)

[2] John 12:32 (KJV).

[3] John 17:22.

[4] George Kennedy Allen Bell was Bishop of Chichester, 1929-1958. He played a prominent part in the Life and Work movement, and facilitated the first meeting of the World Council of Churches in Amsterdam in 1948. He was Chairman of its Central Committee, 1948-1954, and thereafter Honorary President until his death in 1958.

[5] Is this alluding to the foundation of the European Economic Community on March 25, 1957?

[6] The second assembly of the World Council of Churches at Evanston, Illinois, August 1954.

[7] This may refer to the first assembly of the World Council of Churches in Amsterdam in 1948.

Notes Continued

8 In 1947 from the Anglican, Congregationalist, Presbyterian and Methodist churches in southern India.

9 Alfred Lord Tennyson.

10 Alluding to the Blackpool illumination, an annual lights festival in that city since 1879.

11 cf. the hymn 'Jesu thou joy of loving hearts', cento from *Jesu dulcis memoria*, translated by Ray Palmer (1858).

12 John 17:11, 15.

13 cf. the 'Prayer of St. Francis'.

Tamworth
New South Wales

Influence[1]

I am deeply impressed by the women of Australia. Don't underestimate the importance of your contribution both in the past and in the future of this great country. It is always a question of debate: "Who has the greater influence in life – men or women?" Let us say women are more subtle! They are "the power behind the throne"! The whole course of history could have been changed if Pilate had allowed himself to be influenced by his wife when she advised him, "Have nothing to do with that just man."[2] The influence of many great women in many spheres of life is felt by us today.

MRS EMMELINE PANKHURST[3]

As a child I remember the heated campaign in England for 'Votes for Women'. Previously women had no say in the affairs of Government. Mrs. Pankhurst roused the women suffragettes to tremendous endeavour. She harnessed their persuasive powers in speaking in public. Many were imprisoned, some were forcibly fed. They used their power to suffer for the benefit of their cause. During the 1914-1918 war women proved their point – that they were of fundamental importance to their country. They won the vote[4] and their voice has been valuable in elections ever since. Lady Astor was the first female Member of Parliament.[5]

FLORENCE NIGHTINGALE

Florence Nightingale[6] was an Italian-born British nurse in the 19th century. From her earliest years it was apparent that she wanted to relieve suffering. She nursed dolls and then animals. Some of the brightest pages in history tell of her glowing service to the wounded in the Crimean War. Sometimes she stood for 20 hours at a stretch. There were no night nurses but she would go round in the solitary hours with her lamp. Before she took charge, the death rate was 42%. In two months after her appointment, it was down to 2%. She made strenuous efforts to improve hygiene and to ensure the hospital patients had access to fresh air. England sent a Man of War to bring her home, but she actually returned in a French ship. When £50,000 was awarded to her, she used it to found the Nightingale Home for training nurses. Her influence travelled far and wide. At the Sisters' Graduation ceremony at Tamworth Base Hospital, the nurses still take a Florence Nightingale pledge. Like a stone dropped in a pool causing ripples to spread to the circumference, her influence has passed from one generation to another.

ELIZABETH FRY

Elizabeth Fry[7] was one of the chief promoters of Prison Reform. She was a Quaker and she used to visit Newgate Prison in London where she read the Bible to the prisoners, who were held in ghastly conditions. She found that there was no separation of the sexes, and no classification of criminals. They had no religious instruction and no useful employment.[8] All this she was able to persuade the prison authorities to alter.

What a debt of gratitude we owe to these women pioneers! They all drew strength, courage and inspiration from God.

What about our own sphere of influence? We may feel that we can never do what these great women have done. But we have a mighty weapon in our hands to wield – the power of influencing others. Mothers have always had this power, from one generation to another. Thinking of his own mother Monica, St. Augustine said, "Give me the mothers to train and I will change the world."[9] And Mary Sumner, the founder of the Mother's Union, considered that things learnt in childhood are never forgotten.[10] Mothers make the paths for their children to tread all their lives, sometimes unconsciously.

Are we careful enough to see that our older children come under the right influences? I am thinking of their friendships and their choice of entertainment. Are we teaching them the joy of serving other people? Something greater than giving them freedom is the right use of freedom. When young people get into trouble very often it is not their fault but *the fault of their parents.* How can we be sure that our influence is to be the best for our families and in our parishes?

Only by throwing open our hearts and minds to our Saviour Jesus Christ. "He came sweet influence to impart."[11] The things we lack, he alone can give us. Jesus said, "If anyone thirsts, let him come to me and drink. He who believes in me … out of his heart shall flow rivers of living water."[12] Rivers are so vital in every country. Along their banks the richest vegetation grows – the fine trees and the greenest paddocks. It is on the banks of rivers of every country that towns are built and life thrives. They aid communication and the provision of supplies. Rivers have their sources high in the mountains, and so must we have our source in God if our lives are to bring refreshment and growth and life to others.

Jesu, thou joy of loving hearts!
Thou fount of life, thou Light of men!
From the best bliss that earth imparts
We turn unfilled to thee again.[13]

Notes

1 A talk given at the Diocesan Women's Conference in the city of Armidale in 1960 or 1961.

2 Matthew 27:19.

3 Emmeline Pankhurst, 1858-1928.

4 The 'Representation of the People Act 1918' allowed the vote to all men over 21 and to all women over 30 who had minimum property qualifications. In 1928 the 'Representation of the People (Equal Franchise) Act' gave the vote to all women over the age of 21, on equal terms with men.

5 Her constituency was Plymouth Sutton, a seat she held from 1919-1945.

6 Florence Nightingale, 1820-1910.

7 Elizabeth Fry, 1780-1845.

8 cf. "She campaigned for the separation of the sexes, classification of criminals, female supervision of women, and the provision of secular and religious instruction" – *The Concise Oxford Dictionary of the Christian Church*, 2nd rev. edn, ed. by E. A. Livingstone, online version 2013 – speaking of Elizabeth Fry's activity in 1813.

9 A slogan, perhaps, based on the influence Monica had on her son Augustine (354-430), whose writings have had a global impact.

10 Early in the twentieth century the Mothers' Union issued a badge to its members: around an image of the Madonna and Child is a quotation of the first half of Proverbs 22:6: "Train up a child in the way he should go"; lack of space precluded adding the rest of the text, "and when he is old, he will not depart from it."

11 From the hymn 'Our blessed Redeemer, ere he breathed', by Harriet Auber (1829).

12 John 7:37-38.

13 From *Jesu dulcis memoria,* translated by Ray Palmer (1808-1887).

When Evening Falls[1]

On a fine night how quietly and gently the evening falls! Almost imperceptibly the day melts into night. We have often watched in wonder the beauty of the setting sun. The Tamworth hills glow pink with reflected light. Gradually the colours fade into pale bands of green and pink and misty blue, that lie across the rim of the horizon. Then the colours fade out of the sky and darkness falls. The stars, like brilliant diamonds, are scattered upon the deep velvet of the sky. Lights from each home stud the hills like glow-worms. The ethereal moon rises in pale majesty above the hills.

What peace and tranquillity settle upon the earth at evening time! That is God's provision for us at the close of the day. It is just what we need most for the relaxation of our tired bodies and weary minds. In sleep we are restored for another day. One of the loveliest records we have of our Lord's resurrection appearances, written in chapter 24 of St. Luke's Gospel, tells of two disciples walking with him to their home at evening time under a beautiful Eastern sky. As they reached their house, Jesus was about to leave them and pass on, but they constrained him and said, "Stay with us, Lord, for it is towards evening."[2]

They had suffered bereavement and loss. They had felt the keenness of bitter disappointment because things had not gone as they hoped. They had put all their hope in Christ their master to restore the kingdom of Israel and deliver them from the heel of the Roman invader, but they had found that, far from saving them, he had not even been able to save himself from the cruel death of the Cross. So they felt hopeless, their faith was shaken.

Some of us this week have had our faith shaken; we have had our hopes shattered. It is just there that Jesus meets us and goes with us. He will not force an entrance into our homes and hearts. He waits for us to invite him in – "Lord, stay with us for it is towards evening." Let us make this our own prayer tonight. Just as he gives peace and quietness to the earth at night, he will give us peace that shall keep our hearts and minds.

Three things can destroy our peace tonight which our Lord can lift from us if we let him. First of all, there is regret that we cannot undo the mistakes of the past, but our Lord understands all our circumstances and he is ready to give us the peace of his forgiveness. As St. John tells us, "If we confess our sins, he is faithful and just to forgive us our sins, and to cleanse us from all unrighteousness."[3] Remember, tomorrow will be a new day and we can make a fresh start.

Another thing that can spoil our peace tonight is anxiety. Jesus said, "Take no anxious thought for the morrow, for the morrow shall take thought for the things of itself."[4] God is stronger and wiser than we are; we can safely commit our lives and the lives of our loved ones to him.

> *Peace, perfect peace, with loved ones far away*
> *In Jesus' keeping we are safe and they.*[5]

The third thing that can destroy our peace is if we harbour anger or resentment in our hearts against anyone. St. Paul gave us one of the soundest pieces of advice when he said, "Let not the sun go down upon your wrath."[6] If any of us has had a quarrel we must make it up before we go to sleep. "Stay with us, Lord, for it is towards evening."

> *My Lord, my love, my heart's eternal light,*
> *Shine in my heart through the hours of night.*
> *Shine on my thoughts, my very dreams be found*
> *About thy business on some holy ground.*
>
> *Should friendly angel come to meet me there,*
> *Let me not miss him, deaf and unaware,*
> *And if I may, one other prayer I bring:*
> *O Lord, my God, make no long tarrying.*[7]

Notes

[1] Probably an epilogue broadcast over Radio 2TM.
[2] cf. Luke 24:29.
[3] 1 John 1:9.
[4] cf. Matthew 6:34.
[5] From the hymn 'Peace, perfect peace', by Bishop Edward Henry Bickersteth (1875).
[6] Ephesians 4:26.
[7] From the poem 'Before Sleep', by Amy Carmichael. Line 2 normally: 'Shine on Thy lover through the hours of this night.'

The Dew[1]

We are all tired tonight from the heat and toil of the day. The earth outside is parched and dry. We are all in need of refreshment. At this moment, now darkness has fallen, God is sending his unfailing refreshment to the earth – the dew is falling. Tomorrow morning, if we go out early, we shall smell the sweet scent of the earth. The grass and the flowers will sparkle with the drops of dew glistening in the brilliant sunlight. There will be that freshness and exhilaration in the air that comes from a garden drenched with the dew. God gave this wonderful assurance to his prophet: "I will be like the dew to Israel."[2]

If we think of the ways that the dew comes to refresh and wash our earth, we can think too of the way in which God comes to cleanse and refresh our spirits. There is an ancient prayer: "Pour upon them the perpetual dew of thy blessing."[3]

THE DEW FALLS UNSEEN

We are hardly aware of it. God comes to us unseen. His presence with us through his Holy Spirit is unseen. Jesus said the Holy Spirit is like the wind.[4] We cannot see the wind, but we can hear it and feel it, and see the evidences of its power in the bending trees, and the swirling dust and leaves, and the flying spray blown from the great sea waves. We are told that for Moses, the afflictions in Egypt under Pharaoh were made bearable to him because he endured "as seeing him who is invisible".[5] He lived by faith and not by sight.

THE DEW FALLS IN DARKNESS

We all without exception have our dark times. It has been the experience of the saints of all ages that they go through times of darkness and spiritual dryness. But the dew from heaven falls in darkness. I have known many who have experienced the presence of God in a new and more vivid way during illness. Very often, when we are withdrawn from activity, we are given a keener spiritual perception of life, a sense of true values.

I remember the wife of a headmaster in one of our parishes in England telling me of the blessing given to her during a time of darkness when she had undergone a major operation. One night she sent for my husband to come to the hospital because she was in great pain and could not sleep.

Telling me of this afterwards she said to me, "That night your husband put my hand into the hand of God, and the following day, when the nurses lifted me up to dress my wound, I caught sight of myself in the mirror on my dressing table and, suddenly, I saw the crucified Christ bearing the suffering of his wounds for love of us. I knew that he shared my suffering and the suffering of the world." God gave to her the dew of his blessing in darkness.

THE DEW CAN ONLY FALL UPON THINGS THAT ARE STILL

So often the reason that we are not conscious of God's blessing is that we are too busy – rushing about from one appointment to another, rushing to get everything done and leaving what is most important of all undone. Our greatest spiritual blessings will only come to us when we take time to be alone in prayer before God. "Be still, and know that I am God."[6]

THE DEW IS UNFAILING

When there is no rain, still the dew falls. God is an unfailing source of strength and refreshment. Before we go to sleep, let us pray this prayer:

Drop thy still dews of quietness,
Till all our strivings cease;
Take from our souls the strain and stress,
And let our ordered lives confess
The beauty of thy peace.[7]

Notes

[1] Probably an epilogue broadcast over Radio 2TM.

[2] Hosea 14:5.

[3] *The Book of Common Prayer* (1662), Morning Prayer, 'A Prayer for the Clergy and People'.

[4] John 3:8.

[5] Hebrews 11:27.

[6] Psalm 46:10.

[7] From the hymn 'Dear Lord and Father of mankind', by John Greenleaf Whittier (1872).

A Great Rock in a Weary Land[1]

A man will be as a hiding place from the wind, and a cover from the tempest, as rivers of water in a dry place, as the shadow of a great rock in a weary land.

Isaiah 32:2

Recently, during a time of difficulty, this verse has been a great source of strength and comfort to me. We are all fellow travellers in a weary land. There is a great deal in life to make us feel tired. There are so many problems and so many important decisions to make for ourselves and our families. Responsibility makes us tired.

Monotonous, unrewarding work makes us tired as well. Thousands of people think of work as merely a way of earning a living, and an uninteresting one at that. It is said truthfully, "A woman's work is never done." There must be many tired mothers listening tonight who agree with this and wonder how they can face another week of relentless work. Yes, we are all travellers in a weary land.

This particular traveller of whom we read had been travelling for days in blazing heat. His anxious eyes scanned the miles of sandy desert for shade and water. Suddenly his heart lightened as he saw in the distance a landmark – a great rock in a weary land. At last there was hope of shade and relief from the relentless sun, protection from the desert storms. This traveller had often seen people blinded and suffocated by sandstorms. He had seen tents torn to shreds by the wind and palm trees uprooted. But here at last was secure shelter – a rock, immovable, strong and dependable against the most violent storm.

There come times for all of us in life when we are in danger of being completely uprooted; when, for instance, some unexpected shock hits us, such as bereavement, illness or the fear of the unknown either in life or in death. The security we had built round us is shaken – everything seems to be slipping from us. We need desperately a great Rock in a weary land.

St. Paul related in his First Epistle to the Corinthians, chapter 10, how the children of Israel were rescued from intense suffering from exposure and thirst in the desert. God had provided them with a great rock and said to Moses, "I will stand before you there on the rock in Horeb; and you shall strike the rock, and water will come out of it, that the people may drink."[2] Recalling this experience of the Israelites, St. Paul said they "did all drink the same spiritual drink: for they drank of that spiritual rock ... and that Rock was Christ".[3] Christ is our rock, immovable and utterly dependable.

> *Rock of ages, cleft for me,*
> *Let me hide myself in thee;*
> *Let the water and the blood,*
> *From thy riven side which flowed,*
> *Be of sin the double cure:*
> *Cleanse me from its guilt and power.[4]*

Christ can do for me what I cannot do for myself. He can cleanse the very source of my heart from evil. Most of us are so independent. It is all part of our pride. One of the great lessons that trouble and illness teach us is that our ultimate dependence is upon God. We shall find great blessing if, in trouble, we allow ourselves to be driven closer to God for his protection.

Prebendary Carlile,[5] when faced with an infection of the spine necessitating a year on his back, said, "God threw me there on my back that I might look up to him." Baron von Hügel, as spiritual adviser to those who were going through great trouble, said, "Imitate the Arabs. When a sandstorm comes in the desert, they fling themselves on the ground and cover their heads and wait for the storm to pass." He advises, "Never make a decision or take action in a crisis," but wait in quiet dependence upon God, stayed upon his strength.[6]

Before we go to sleep, may we turn afresh to Christ, our great Rock in a weary land, and press our weakness close to his strength, and win new power for the morrow, stayed on the rock of his faithfulness.

Notes

[1] Probably an epilogue broadcast over Radio 2TM.

[2] Exodus 17:6.

[3] 1 Corinthians 10:4 (KJV).

[4] From the hymn of Augustus Montague Toplady (1763).

[5] Prebendary Wilson Carlile, founder of the Church Army. "Throughout his life, Wilson suffered from spinal weakness. 'God threw me on my back so that I could look up to him more,' he quipped." (*Share It!*, the magazine of the Church Army, Spring/Summer 2017).

Notes Continued

[6] This is a fair summary of von Hügel's actual words: "I am travelling on a camel across a huge desert ... Hurricanes of wind will come, unforeseen, tremendous. What to do then? ... Dismount from the camel, fall prostrate face downwards on the sand, covering your head with your cloak. And lie thus, an hour, three hours, half a day: the sandstorm will go, and you will arise, and continue your journey as if nothing had happened." He is talking of images from nature that have helped him in difficult times. Shortly after, he says that in such situations, "there is each time one crucial point – to form no conclusions, to take no decisions, to change nothing during such crises ... To turn gently to other things, to maintain a vague, general attitude of resignation ... It is far, far more God who must hold us, than we who must hold him." *Letters to a Niece*, April 21, 1920.

Remembrance[1]

We all like to be remembered by those who love us. By remembrance our relatives and friends centre their love and thought upon us and give us strength. Remembrance is so often connected in our minds with the closing hours of life. How many mourners we have watched throwing into the open grave their sprigs of rosemary for remembrance.

As we come to the end of another day, let us think of the closing hours of life of a man we call 'the dying thief'. In that short time of crucifixion, his heart had been touched by the Saviour of the World, revealing on that central Cross the limits to which love will go. In faith he cried out, "Lord, remember me when you come into your kingdom."[2] First of all, in those words, he recognised Christ as a King of a kingdom not of this world.

Then, he realised that death had no power over him, that Christ was indestructible. He had been profoundly moved by our Lord's reaction to suffering, so vastly different from that of the average human being. In his ears still rang, above the metallic thud of the nails being driven through those gentle hands, the prayer of compassion that our Lord had prayed for his enemies, "Father, forgive them, for they know not what they do."[3] He had watched with amazement Christ's last loving provision for his mother as he had committed her and St. John into each other's keeping. From that hour, St. John took her to his own home saving her the anguish of watching his last agony when darkness fell upon his soul and upon the whole earth. So, watching this monarch die (who thought only of the needs of others and not of his own suffering) brought to birth faith in this man's heart – "Lord, remember me..."

How essential it is for us to be remembered by our Lord tonight, and always, to have his forgiveness for the things in us which have grieved his Holy Spirit. We need, too, to have his loving kindness – "for the heart of the eternal is most wonderfully kind".[4] Our Lord's response to our need and to our faith is instantaneous: "Today you will be with me in Paradise."[5] We have assurance of eternal life, assurance of being with Christ beyond "the changes and chances of this fleeting world".[6] May we make this our prayer of faith tonight: "Lord, remember me."

In the closing hours of our Lord's life, he too asked for remembrance. He made a trysting place where all his disciples could come and meet him, a place where our spirits also can commune with his Spirit, where the rising sap and life of the True Vine can pass into us as his branches.[7]

He said, "This is my body – do this in remembrance of me."[8] He, too, longs for our constant remembrance. Have we forgotten him today or have we made time to remember him? Before you go to sleep tonight remember him. Remember his great love for you, his tender mercy; commit yourself and your family in the prayer he taught us from the Cross: "Father, into your hands, I commit my spirit."[9]

And tomorrow, when we wake up and start another week, let us take up our tasks afresh and do them better than we have ever done them before – in remembrance of him.

Notes

1. Probably an epilogue broadcast over Radio 2TM during Passiontide.
2. Luke 23:42.
3. Luke 23:34.
4. From the hymn 'Souls of men! Why will ye scatter?', by Frederick William Faber (Oratory Hymns, 1854).
5. Luke 23:43.
6. Collect at the evening service 'Compline'.
7. cf. John 15:1-8.
8. Luke 22:19.
9. Luke 23:46.

In the Hand of God[1]

All our lives, from babyhood to old age, it matters very much to us the kind of hands into which we fall. As parents, we are very careful of the hands in which we place our children. We think of the many hands that have touched our lives: the strong ones, the weak ones, the rough ones, and the grasping ones – out to extract every penny. We remember the capable hands in which we have felt safe and confident, and the soothing hand of motherhood easing pain and banishing fears. All through life, our hands are used either for self or for the service of others.

THINK OF THE HEALING HANDS OF OUR LORD JESUS

How expressive they were of the love of God! His hands were only used to bless. That is what he wants our hands to be used for every day – for blessing, for healing and for strengthening. Think of his healing hands. He took the little sick girl by the hand and healed her.[2] He took the blind man by the hand and laid his hands upon his eyes and healed him.[3] He touched the untouchable – the leper.[4] His healing hand was laid upon countless lives, and virtue went out of him to them.[5] He brought wholeness of body, mind and spirit, and put invalids back into lives of active service for him.

In our Lord's hands the most inadequate supply was made enough. Even a little boy's lunch was made enough to feed a multitude.[6] He took a child into his loving hands and forever consecrated his childhood.[7] He took a fallen woman and lifted her up to lead a dedicated life.[8] Jesus took bread, ordinary daily food and lifted it up to be the sacrament of his life broken for us. Similarly, he took the cup of wine in his hands and lifted it up to be a sacrament of his lifeblood outpoured for us for the remission of our sins.[9]

THINK OF THE WOUNDED HANDS OF JESUS

The Romans looked for the mailed hand of force – they found instead the nailed hand of love. What a terrible thing it seems that those beautiful hands of Christ, that never did anything but bless and heal and comfort, were wounded! He fell into the rough and cruel hands of sinful men. "See in his hands the print of the nails."[10] In the words of a favourite hymn:

> *See from his head, his hands, his feet,*
> *Sorrow and love flow mingling down;*

Did e'er such love and sorrow meet,
Or thorns compose so rich a crown?[11]

Love went to its furthest limit when his hands were stretched out on the Cross to embrace the world.

LET HIS LAST PRAYER BE OURS

"Into your hands I commit my spirit."[12] Let our response to his great love be complete. We cannot put ourselves or our loved ones into better hands than into the hands of God. "Therefore, humble yourselves under the mighty hand of God, that he may exalt you in due time."[13] "The souls of the righteous are in the hand of God and there shall no torment touch them."[14]

Tonight, before we go to sleep, let us put our hands into the hands of our Saviour asking him to make them healing hands in his service.

Lord, take my hands,
And let them move at the impulse of thy love.[15]

Notes

[1]   Probably an epilogue broadcast over Radio 2TM.
[2]   Mark 5:41.
[3]   Mark 8:23-25.
[4]   Mark 1:41.
[5]   Luke 6:17-19.
[6]   Mark 6:30-44.
[7]   Mark 9:36.
[8]   Luke 7:36-50, John 8:1-11.
[9]   Matthew 26:26-28.
[10] John 20:25.
[11] From 'When I survey the wondrous Cross', by Isaac Watts (*Hymns and Spiritual Songs,* 1707).
[12] Luke 23:36.
[13] 1 Peter 5:6.
[14] Wisdom 3:1.
[15] From the hymn 'Take my life, and let it be', by Frances Ridley Havergal (1874).

Light

This week in Tamworth we are celebrating the sixth anniversary of the Festival of Light.[1] One of my memories as a child was of the street lamp lighter. The streets were lit by gas and when darkness began to fall, we used to stand at the window, eager to see the lamplighter riding his bicycle up our road. He used to hold a long pole in his hand; it had a hook at the end with which to pull down the catch and turn on the gas light. We used to mark his progress down the road by the lamps he had lit.

Sir Harry Lauder, the Scottish comedian, speaking once at an eminent businessmen's lunch, told of his own pleasure at watching the lamplighter. After a short pause, he said to them, "Your business and mine, my friends, is so to live that after we have gone our way through life, we shall leave a trail of light that will guide the steps of those who otherwise might walk in darkness."[2]

This week many of us have been remembering those whose lives have been to us as lights, revealing the right path for us to take in life. Some children were asked the question, "What is a Saint?" Quickly the reply came: "One through whom the light of God shines." Most of us have known someone who had, or has, that particular radiance about them. It is not so much what they say but what they *are* that counts. "The path of the just is like the shining sun, that shines ever brighter unto the perfect day."[3]

Our Lord described this radiance in St. John the Baptist when he said of him, "He was a burning and a shining light."[4] We thank God for all those who have lighted up the things of God for us – a godly mother, a godly sister, or husband, or wife, or friend, or child.

The saints have one thing in common, the sense that they are not saints but sinners in God's presence – "they who fain would serve thee best are conscious most of wrong within".[5] They are all filled with a sense of need and inadequacy, and they all turn to the same Source for light. "God is light, and in him is no darkness at all."[6] It is a great help to hold on to that truth when we are going through periods of great darkness.

In our Lord's time in Jerusalem, the Jews kept their own Festival of Light in October. It is called the Feast of Tabernacles. To commemorate God's leading of the Children of Israel through the wilderness by a pillar of fire, they lighted four great candlesticks in the Women's Court of the

Temple.[7] It was at this ceremony that our Lord stood up and cried out this great declaration: "I am the Light of the World. He who follows me shall not walk in darkness, but shall have the light of life."[8]

If our minds are darkened with problems and doubts, Christ can dispel that darkness with his light. If we do not know which way to turn, he can illuminate our path with his light and give us divine guidance. A child was so frightened at night and kept calling his mother up to stay with him. Patiently the mother said to him, "God is with you and you are safe." But the child soon called again. "What is it?" the mother asked. "Oh, Mother," said the little boy, "I wish God had a face!"

Christ has given us the face of God. "For it is the God who commanded light to shine out of darkness, who has shone in our hearts to give the light of the knowledge of the glory of God in the face of Jesus Christ."[9]

> *Turn your eyes upon Jesus,*
> *look full in his wonderful face,*
> *and the things of earth shall grow strangely dim,*
> *in the light of his glory and grace.*[10]

He will lead us safely through this life and beyond to the Celestial City, where we are told there is no need for the light of the sun, neither of the moon, to shine in it "for the glory of God illuminated it. The Lamb is its light."[11]

Notes

[1] The Festival of Light was set up in 1958 as an annual celebration of Tamworth as the 'City of Light', having been the first city in Australia to use street lights powered by a municipal electricity company, seventy years before, on November 8, 1888. This talk was delivered in the first week of November 1963.

[2] From various Internet sources it is clear Sir Harry Lauder often told about the old lamplighter in his village and his trail of lighted lamps. He used this example to encourage his listeners so to live that they would leave a trail of lights (goodness) for others to follow. See for instance:

www.creators.com/read/classic-zig-ziglar/09/16/teaching-by-parables
(14 Sep. 2016).

[3] Proverbs 4:18.

[4] John 5:35 (KJV).

[5] From the hymn 'At even, ere the sun was set', by Henry Twells (1868).

[6] 1 John 1:5.

Notes Continued

7 Mishnah, *Sukkah* 5.2-3; for more details see:

   https://en.wikibooks.org/wiki/Hebrew_Roots/Holy_Days/.../Hoshanna_Rab
   ba

8 John 8:12. 7:53-8:11 appears to be an editorial intrusion into the text of Scripture here; its style of writing is not that of the author of John's Gospel, and some Greek manuscripts insert it after Luke 21:38. It seems fair then to deduce that John 8:12 follows on from 7:52 and so still relates to the Feast of Tabernacles.

9 2 Corinthians 4:6.

10 By Helen Howath Lemmel (1922). Mother learnt this chorus at CSSM Bude, and it was ever after a favourite of hers.

11 Revelation 21:23.

Witnesses[1]

You shall be witnesses to me.

Acts 1:8

The importance of being a witness was brought home to me when I was the sole witness to a road accident. I had to make a statement to the police and appear as a witness in court. On my evidence hung the fate of the driver. In our Courts of Law, witnesses hold in their hand the Bible to take the oath, "I swear by Almighty God that I will speak the truth, the whole truth and nothing but the truth."[2]

Our Lord depended on the faithful witness of his disciples to the truth. He said, "You are my witnesses"[3] – both to him who is the truth[4] and to his resurrection.[5] If it had not been for their recorded witness, we would not now hold the Bible in our hands. There is a legend that the angel Gabriel once asked Christ, "What plans have you made for your Church?" Jesus replied, "I have left my disciples to witness." Then Gabriel asked, "What other plans have you made?" "I have made no other plans," replied Jesus.

St. John shone as a witness. In the first verses of his first letter we read:

> *That which was from the beginning, which we have heard, which we have seen with our eyes, which we have looked upon, and our hands have handled, of the Word of Life; for the Life was manifested and we have seen it, and bear witness...*[6]

We have all come to our present faith through the witness of those who lived in the past. Let us think back to the witnesses to Christ in our own lives. For many of us, our first witness will have been our mother, or someone who acted as mother to us. It was her witness that planted our feet on the right paths – telling us Bible stories about Jesus, taking us to church. Mary Sumner was a shining witness to God. She speaks of the witness of her own mother as "the angel in the house",[7] who influenced the whole of her children's lives by early morning Bible readings in her own room. Mary Sumner emphasised the unique opportunities of mothers as witnesses in their own homes. "Train up a child in the way he should go: and when he is old, he will not depart from it."[8] He may depart for a while... but he will come back. You will of course need to exert some discipline and expect obedience. Some of you are lone witnesses. God needs you all the more.

God urgently needs his witnesses today in the world. Some of you are not mothers – you are still needed as witnesses to our Lord in supporting his teaching against the tide of the world. Support every movement that strengthens family life and the stability of marriage. To you who teach religious instruction, Jesus says, "You are my witnesses."[9] So often it is not so much the children who are to blame as the parents. Stay with them, communicate with them, don't segregate yourself too much from them.

Christ needs his witnesses in the world just now. We ourselves must be a 'Festival of Light'![10] "When the enemy comes in like a flood, I will lift up my standard against him."[11]

Notes

[1] A talk to the Mothers' Union in Tamworth.

[2] The correct wording of an oath in a court of law is, "I swear that the evidence I shall give, shall be the truth, the whole truth and nothing but the truth, so help me God." There is alternative wording for those who do not wish to invoke the name of God.

[3] cf. Luke 24:48, John 15:27, Acts 1:8.

[4] John 1:14, cf. John 14:6.

[5] Acts 2:32, 1 Corinthians 15:4-8.

[6] 1 John 1:1-2 (KJV).

[7] See *Mary Sumner*, by Horatia Erskine, p.7.

[8] Proverbs 22:6.

[9] cf. Acts 1:8.

[10] See earlier Tamworth talk 'Light', note 1.

[11] cf. Isaiah 59:19.

Mother and Child[1]

We are thinking about a young mother in Palestine in the lifetime of our Lord. Palestine had much in common with this country – sunshine, heat, sudden storms. There were citrus fruits, vines and sheep. To a large extent, there was an open-air lifestyle. This mother's little son wanted to spend the day out-of-doors. He wanted to watch and hear the wonderful preacher of the open air. He talked about things a child loved and understood – the seed, the harvest, the lilies of the field, the sparrows. The mother thought, "He'll get hungry out all day in the open air – I must pack up his picnic basket." Lovingly she put in the five small barley loaves and the two small cooked fish for his lunch. He kissed her and waved goodbye, and climbed the mountain path and joined the crowd.

What a crowd! Five thousand people! The little boy slipped nimbly between the grown-ups until he was close to Jesus and his disciples. Andrew bent down and put his arm protectingly round his shoulders. Perhaps he offered to hold the picnic basket. They were all getting hungry... What should they do? Apologetically Andrew told Jesus, "There is a lad here with his lunch – but what is that among so many?" Jesus took what the loving mother had given her son, the provision she had made for him, and he blessed it... and fed that vast company.

Mothers, what are you packing in your children's basket to take with them on life's way? What provisions are you making for them, the kind of things that we can ask Jesus to bless and use as a blessing for others? What are we providing in our own homes? Worldly possessions only? Or also spiritual qualities with which they will bless and enrich others in life?

Mary Sumner was the kind of mother who packed into her children's lives the things that our Lord could bless and use. She realised that the home was the greatest influence in the formation of character. She believed that the home must be built upon love, our love crowned by the love of God. We pray, "Make us faithful wives and loving mothers."[2] We need of course also to be 'loving wives'! It is not so much a matter of what we do, but the way we do it. Building our homes on love is not in any way related to wealth. "Better is a dinner of herbs where love is than a fatted calf with hatred."[3] Love is a tender plant and needs a lot of tending. In our Marriage Service we promise "to love and to cherish". The nature of love is to give and not to get. Wives and mothers have plenty of opportunities for giving!

92

Mary Sumner wanted to awaken in all mothers a sense of responsibility in the training of their children for heaven. Listen to what she said:

> We must train our children in the dawn of life, these first years are so unspeakably precious and the mother and father form the atmosphere of the home, they make or mar the character of their children. Every life is more or less formed inside a home either for blessing or the contrary. It has been said that to fill the mind with beautiful images is the best thing that can be done to educate little children and what in the world is so beautiful to a child as the personality of our Lord Jesus Christ and his infinite love for children?[4]

Children have a natural instinct for God. They have trust in us and faith in God. "What we mould in wax, we cast in stone."[5]

Mary Sumner hoped to organise in every place a band of mothers who will unite in prayer, and seek by their example to lead their families in God's ways. We can only make the right provision for our children through prayer, which is not just asking for things, but drawing near to God as he draws near to us[6] – absorbing him. It is a most beautiful sight to find a husband and wife praying together. Don't be afraid to let your children see you on your knees.

Notes

[1] A talk given to Mothers' Union members with young children, based on John 6:1-14. It was probably delivered in Tamworth or perhaps South Australia.

[2] Included in the earliest daily prayer of Mary Sumner's mothers' group in the parish of Old Alresford is the petition, "Help me to be a faithful wife and a loving mother." Moyse, *History of the Mothers' Union*, p.253.

[3] Proverbs 15:17.

[4] From *Mary Sumner*, by Erskine, pp. 14-15, reproduced by Mother here verbatim except for interchanging 'mother' and 'father' in line 2.

[5] This maxim may have come from Mary Sumner.

[6] James 4:8.

Prayer[1]

This is the confidence that we have in him, that if we ask anything according to his will, he hears us.

1 John 5:14

The Mothers' Union's 'Third Object' of prayer should be the first![2] Mary Sumner was a great woman of prayer, and the Mothers' Union was born and nurtured in prayer.

PRAYER IS NOT JUST ASKING FOR THINGS

It is not the bending down of God's will to ours, but the raising up of our wills to his. Our son Andrew once said, "I think it is terrible the way we order God about!" We pray daily the perfect prayer, "Your will be done on earth as it is in heaven." Heaven is the place where everything and everyone is in harmony with the will of God. When God's will is done on earth, we shall have heaven on earth. Prayer to be answered must be according to his will. St. John says, "This is the confidence that we have in him, that if we ask anything *according to his will*, he hears us." St. Paul measured his life by what he called "the perfect, acceptable will of God".[3]

PRAYER CHANGES US

A student at College said, "It was not my circumstances that needed changing but I who needed changing."[4] The natural reaction of Ananias, when he was told to go and lay his hands on Saul, was, "Not on *him*, Lord! He's been wrecking the Church. He's no good." But our Lord saw what was happening to Saul and replied, "He is praying."[5] It was while he was praying that he was being made usable. It is in prayer that our wrong attitudes towards God, our circumstances and each other become changed and we become usable to God. God told Ananias that Saul was "a chosen vessel of mine".[6] His attitude changed from doing what he thought was right to, "Lord, what do you want me to do?" Are there unanswered prayers? Prayers must be according to God's will. So, "no" can be an answer.

As breathing is to the body, so prayer is to the soul. We cannot live spiritually without it. Much illness is cured by holding the injured part of the body in concentrated sunlight or under infrared lamps. "God is light and in him is no darkness at all."[7] In prayer, we open our hearts and minds to the penetrating, healing light of God and we hold others in his light too.

WE MUST KEEP A TIME FOR PRAYER

Father Andrew[8] said, "Fence off a bit of each day for God." Nothing gets so crowded out as prayer and quietness. At a School of Prayer, one lady said her only time and place for prayer was in the laundry, where she got away from the family! Father John Lewis said, "We have to have proper meal times. We can't live on nibbles of food all day, so we have to have a time for prayer."[9] The actual time is for each individual to decide. Early morning is good for some but impossible for others. For many mothers, the best time is when the children have gone to school and the husband to work. With a young babe, it is when the child is put to sleep. Confide in your little children that you want to be quiet. Let them draw or crayon while you are quiet.

If you have wandering thoughts, turn them into prayer. The Holy Spirit may be guiding our thoughts. Prayer is the ascent of the soul to God. Use whatever helps your soul ascend. A very simple plan is the four 'P's: *Preparation, Penitence, Praise* and *Petition.*

PREPARATION

We can't just jump into prayer. We need a minute or two of recollection of the presence of God. "Be still, and know that I am God."[10] "Let go and let God." Read verses from the Psalms, St. John's Gospel or the short epistles in a new translation: Ephesians, Galatians, Philippians etc.

PENITENCE

We could say, "Cleanse me from secret faults,"[11] or, "Create in me, O God, a clean heart and renew a right spirit within me,"[12] or use a Lent collect.

PRAISE

Again, use the psalms, or praise God in his creation, or say the Gloria.

PETITION

This is the time for lifting others into God's light.

Notes

[1] A talk to a Mothers' Union group.
[2] The Third Object of the Mothers' Union is: "To maintain a worldwide fellowship of Christians united in prayer, worship and service."

Notes Continued

3   cf. Romans 12:2.

4   A reminiscence from Ridgelands Bible College days perhaps.

5   cf. Acts 9:10-15.

6   Acts 9:15.

7   1 John 1:5.

8   Henry Ernest Hardy (1869-1946) was an English Anglican priest and friar, who co-founded the Society of Divine Compassion to work with the poor in the East End of London, and took the name 'Father Andrew'. He was a prolific author of devotional writings, some in the form of poems. He also wrote plays and was a talented painter.

9   We have not traced this man.

10   Psalm 46:10.

11   Psalm 19:12.

12   cf. Psalm 51:10.

Introducing Children to God[1]

Often young mothers ask, "How soon can I teach my child about God?" The answer is:

> *There cannot be a conscious beginning because your own relationship with God, your knowledge of him, your own prayer life and what you are, must from the first moment of the child's life teach him something about God.*[2]

Thomas Carlyle said, "[My] first and most lasting religious experience was the sight of my mother on her knees."[3] The prayer life of the child unfolds from the life of the mother.

Prayer is the language of the soul, the way we talk or commune with God. In some degree we have to master the language of prayer before we can teach it. We couldn't bear our children to grow up dumb because we never took the trouble to teach them to talk. Their souls will be dumb if we haven't taught them to pray.

Prayer is our preparation for life. It is the time when we forge the links of our life with the great unseen forces of God. It is a time of withdrawal from the many claims made upon us physically and mentally – a spiritual recuperation. It is a time of quietness and stillness. "Be still, and know that I am God."[4] The dew only falls upon things that are still. Get your Quiet Time when you can – early or midday – but by any means get it.

Let your child grow up knowing that to have a Quiet Time is as natural and as necessary as having a meal. Take them into your confidence and pray with them over family difficulties. One child said to his mother, "I believe in God because of the way he answers your prayers."

What should be the time for prayer with your children? It must be when you are free to be with them, morning as well as evening. You must arrange the time in the evening to fit in with all the many happenings then. Use pictures as a help when your children are tiny, to focus their minds. Later, create mental pictures by Bible study.

For prayer itself:

- First, be quiet with them, just thinking of God and loving him, which is adoration.

- Guide them, but let them be as free as possible in their thanksgivings.
- Suggest people in need of prayers, and let them do so too.
- On the matter of protection, you can instil into their minds the thought that God is the creator and lover of all that he has made. He is also the helper of all who are in need, and the protector of all who put their trust in him.

Older children love to make their own Prayer Books. Don't let their prayers become mechanical. Point out they would not say the same thing over and over again to their (earthly) father. Vary the prayers you use with them and teach them new ones. Explain the meaning of the Lord's Prayer.

Notes

[1] A talk to young mothers.

[2] The source of this quotation has not yet been traced but may be a speech or writing of Mary Sumner.

[3] Mother's script reads "The first and most lasting…" Thomas Carlyle (1795-1881) was a Scottish philosopher, writer and mathematician. His parents, to whom he was devoted, were strict Calvinists. His mother taught him to read and his father taught him arithmetic. Later in life he lost his faith but adopted a form of deism. Perhaps Carlyle shared this reminiscence about his mother with Mary Sumner, as he was known to her and her husband – Olive Parker, *For the Family's Sake: A History of the Mothers' Union, 1876-1976* (Mowbray, 1975), p.9.

[4] Psalm 46:10.

The Week of the Cross[1]

Then, six days before the Passover, Jesus came to Bethany, where Lazarus was who had been dead, whom He had raised from the dead. There they made Him a supper; and Martha served, but Lazarus was one of those who sat at the table with Him. Then Mary took a pound of very costly oil of spikenard, anointed the feet of Jesus, and wiped His feet with her hair. And the house was filled with the fragrance of the oil. But one of His disciples, Judas Iscariot, Simon's son, who would betray Him, said, "Why was this fragrant oil not sold for three hundred denarii and given to the poor?" This he said, not that he cared for the poor, but because he was a thief, and had the money box; and he used to take what was put in it. But Jesus said, "Let her alone; she has kept this for the day of My burial. For the poor you have with you always, but Me you do not have always." Now a great many of the Jews knew that He was there; and they came, not for Jesus' sake only, but that they might also see Lazarus, whom He had raised from the dead. But the chief priests plotted to put Lazarus to death also, because on account of him many of the Jews went away and believed in Jesus.

John 12:1-11[2]

Six days before his death, Jesus chose to go into a simple home where he was loved. He turned towards Bethany for the comfort and refreshment he knew that such a home could give him. It was a place where he was best understood, a place of rest. He wanted the companionship of his friends before he faced his foes. All were transformed by Jesus, except Judas. Let us see a few of them. The home was that of Simon, a leper, an intimate friend of Martha and Mary.

MARTHA

We learn that Martha served. Last time she had prepared a meal for Jesus[3] she had been encumbered about by her serving duties, but now she had learned to serve quietly. She had won peace and calm from her Lord.

LAZARUS

Lazarus was also there. He had been raised from the dead,[4] and sat at supper with them. His presence almost spoilt the privacy of that meal, because we are told, "Many people, hearing that Jesus was there, came, not for Jesus' sake only, but also to see Lazarus."[5] These were the curious ones; they had ulterior motives.

MARY

Mary was nearest to Jesus. Twice in the Gospels we have seen her, and each time she is at the feet of Jesus. She had deep intuition of what these last days were meaning to Jesus. She saw what it cost him to set his face to go to Jerusalem. She anticipated the sufferings he would endure. She saw all suffering as a faint reflection of his own. He was entering into the deepest of all human experience – suffering of both mind and body. "He has borne our griefs and carried our sorrows."[6] The beauty and scent of the rose are accompanied by thorns! Mary knew that his suffering would be greater than all others because he loved more deeply than any other. Deep love goes hand in hand with deep suffering.

How did she respond to his love and his sufferings for her soul? She took an alabaster box,[7] "exceedingly precious". It was Arabian perfume. She took what was most precious to her. It cost 300 pence. When the wage was one penny a day,[8] it was nearly a year's wages. She broke the transparent box and poured the contents over Jesus' feet. Her love was responding to his love. Can we take what is exceedingly precious to us and pour it out? We must not keep what is precious to ourselves. Maybe it is a person. What is our response to the love poured out for us on the Cross?

Mary made her offering in time. It was her last opportunity. Jesus defended her action by saying, "She has kept this for the day of my burial."[9] She was not among the women who embalmed Jesus' body after he had died. She did not leave it till it was too late. We often do. She had no regrets.

The house was filled with the fragrance of the ointment. The atmosphere of the entire home was pervaded by Mary's love for Christ. Worship must *fill our lives,* not just be kept for Sundays. Every room – the living room, the kitchen, the children's room – must be affected by it. It changes the atmosphere. Things are no longer drudgery because they are done "for Jesus' sake".[10] This is the practical outcome of devotion to him. Of Mary it was true to say, "She has done what she could."[11]

Editors' Note: To the script of this address a letter was attached from Jean Norgate of the China Inland Mission, written from Turramurra, New South Wales. It is dated 3 July 1964:

Dear Mrs Daunton-Fear,

After hearing you speak at the Annual Mothers' Union Service last week, I just thought I would like to tell you how much I enjoyed your lovely message, it was a real blessing and challenge to me.

I have heard of the great work you and your husband are doing in Tamworth and I trust there will be much fruit in the days to come.

Thanking you for coming to Sydney,

Yours sincerely,

Jean Norgate

Notes

[1] An address to the Annual Meeting of the Mothers' Union in Sydney Diocese in June 1964. 700 were present and the Archbishop's wife was in the chair. (This information is recorded in Mother's handwriting on a letter from Jean Norgate she received afterwards – printed here after this talk.)

[2] Most of this talk is based on John 12:1-11, but Mother has sought to reconcile this passage with the story of the anointing in Mark 14:3-9 (cf. Matthew 26:6-13) by locating the incident in the house of Simon the Leper and saying the perfume was in an 'alabaster jar'. Many indeed think the two accounts are variants of one original story.

[3] Luke 10:38-42.

[4] John 11:38-44.

[5] cf. John 12:9.

[6] Isaiah 53:4.

[7] This detail is from the account of the anointing of Jesus in Mark 14:3 and Matthew 26:7.

[8] "300 pence" and "a penny a day" are from the King James Version. Some versions prefer the original *denarius.*

[9] John 12:7.

[10] cf. the hymn 'Teach me, my God and King', by George Herbert (1633).

[11] Mark 14:8.

Adelaide

Time for My Neighbour[1]

Time is something that is given to us all. Unlike money, we all have it in equal amount. It is a most precious commodity. We can either waste it or use it to its fullest advantage. The time we waste is never given back to us. It is gone for ever! Like opportunity, it has to be grasped and used at once. As there can be a squandering of money, so there is a squandering of time.

THE RIGHT TIME

First of all, my time needs to be given to God for *his* use. When our time is governed by the hand of God, there is a right time for everything.

Read Ecclesiastes 3:1-8.

Our human life is governed by times and seasons and by days and nights. Our Lord entered into this fully at his Incarnation when he came, as he did, "in the fullness of time".[2] All his life, he was conscious of moving towards a "final hour".[3] When things looked as if his arrest was imminent, he knew that the time was not ripe and told them, "My hour is not yet come."[4] Perfect timing was essential.

Many of our failures in our efforts to serve God are due to our trying to 'force the pace' and to do things when the time is not ripe. We need guidance in prayer, both individually and in groups.

PRIORITIES OF TIME

If we are not to waste time, our priorities must be right. Our love of our neighbours and our preparedness to give them time springs from our love of God and the time we give to him. The two are inseparable. St. John in his first epistle says so simply, "He who loves God must love his brother also."[5] The universal brotherhood of man comes from the universal fatherhood of God.

The Jews were given these two great priorities in life: love of God, and love of our neighbour. When our Lord was asked by a lawyer, "Which is the Great Commandment?" he gave the answer, "You shall love the Lord your God with all your heart, and with all your soul, and with all your mind."[6] Here he was quoting directly from Deuteronomy 6:5. He went on, "This is the first and great commandment. And the second is like it, 'You shall love your neighbour as yourself.' On these two commandments hang all the Law and the Prophets." Here Jesus was quoting from Leviticus 19:18.

But the Jew only thought of his neighbour as 'the children of his own people'. For him, there was a racial limitation. Jesus dealt with this matter in the story of the Good Samaritan in Luke 10:30-37. This parable followed immediately after Luke's account of Jesus giving the two great commandments.[7] The Samaritan was not called 'good' in the Gospel, *we* have added that adjective.

The whole trend of this parable shows that to Jesus our neighbour means *any human being of any race within reach of our help.* In the Old Testament, the Hebrew word for "neighbour"[8] gives the idea of fellowship much more than of proximity. It is not meant to be just the family next door, though if their need arises, they become our neighbours in the deeper sense.

HOW MUCH TIME?

God does not ask of us so much time for our neighbours that we neglect our own families. He only asks for that which we can give and not that which, because of our family commitments, we cannot give.

In the case of a mother with young children, the time which she can give to her neighbour must fit in with her care and routine for her own children. Her sphere of activity will be within her own home, or very close to her own home. I remember a young priest's wife who invited someone living alone in to tea with her every week. The Samaritan took the poor wounded man to an inn to be taken care of. I think that very often that inn can be the rectory. We have often said we live in a public house, and usually our husbands can be trusted to bring in our neighbours! If we, in our love for God, turn our own rectories into inns for wounded and sick souls, we shall learn to be ready day and night for emergencies. We must see those souls as those "for whom Christ died".[9]

When we were in Tamworth, New South Wales, we once received a telephone call from the Base Hospital asking us if we could take care of a young mother whose child had just died under anaesthetic. At moments like that, I think we are called upon to lay everything else aside, to get a friend to mind our children, if they are small, or put the eldest child in charge of the younger ones, and to give ourselves to the one in need. It is fatal to let them think that we haven't time for them. As in an inn, usually hot drinks are needed to help them get over their immediate shock. A hot meal given in loving kindness can be sacramental of the love of God. The cups of cold water given to our Lord are usually cups of tea or coffee![10] The thought that he accepts these offerings transforms our actions: "In as much as you did it to one of the least of my brethren, you did it to me."[11]

It is good for children to grow up in a home where people are brought in to be comforted. Here are sown in their hearts the first seeds of compassion. They learn to think of other people and to do little things for them with their mother, and for Jesus' sake. A young mother told me that she had always seen her mother making soup and light meals for the old and sick, and so she quite naturally did the same thing when she married, and taught her children to do so. Children have their own way of comforting the old and lonely ones and should be encouraged to do so.

Being a Samaritan means that we shall be called upon to bind up many wounds. We are privileged to share our husband's life in a unique way and to share his ordination.[12] We share the very fabric of their lives. Acts of simple kindness are one of the greatest means of evangelism. If we live our lives close to God, then those we help to serve will be brought close to him as well. Those whose lives radiate the love of God can be the very hem of his garment that those in need can touch in faith.[13] People will judge the Church by our actions.

Bereavement is one of the wounds we are always being called upon to bind up very gently. Loneliness is another such wound. Lonely people love to feel needed; perhaps they can be invited to join a church working party of some sort. Then there are young people living away from home for the first time. They often need a 'home from home'. Those of us who can't be away from home for long, can give time to our neighbours within the framework of our parish. People who feel 'shut in' in their own homes can be fetched and driven to services. Young mothers in Tamworth used to arrange musical afternoons and tea for them, fetching and taking them home.

When our families are grown up, we can give time to our neighbours further away from our own homes. We can engage in hospital and sick visiting in the same way that 'Good Samaritan' and 'In as Much Guilds' do. And we mustn't forget the ministry of letter-writing to the lonely. There is only one stipulation: we must not make ourselves so tired that we cannot be a comfort to our own families.

At the end of his life, the Psalmist was able to say to the Lord, "My times are in your hand."[14] If we live daily with our time offered to God, then we too will have confidence for our ultimate destiny and will be able to say, "My times are in your hand," and trust in the perfect timing of God.

Notes

1   A talk or talks given in April 1967, probably to clergy wives, at the Retreat House, Belair, Adelaide.
2   cf. Galatians 4:4.
3   John 12:27, 17:1.
4   cf. John 7:30.
5   1 John 4:21.
6   Matthew 22:37.
7   Luke 10:25-29.
8   *Rea.*
9   Romans 14:15, 1 Corinthians 8:11.
10 cf. Mark 9:41.
11 cf. Matthew 25:40.
12 Today, with the ordination of women, we need to speak of sharing our *spouse's* life.
13 cf. Luke 8:43-44.
14 Psalm 31:15.

The Upper Room (I)[1]

We all pay special attention to the last things said and done by our loved ones just before they passed from this world. Holy Week is set aside so that we may think about the last words and actions of our Lord. St. John, in chapters 13-17 of his Gospel, as it were, lifts a curtain for us to see into the Upper Room where our Lord spent those last hours with his disciples before his arrest. We have come aside from all the things and people who usually occupy our minds to centre our thoughts upon our Lord in this Upper Room in preparation for Holy Week.

In many Jewish homes an upstairs room, which went right across the house, was kept for entertaining guests. Some were large enough to seat 120 people. The Upper Room where the Last Supper took place was probably in the home of the parents of John Mark.[2]

- It was the Upper Room where the disciples met after the Crucifixion (with the doors shut for fear of the Jews). Our Lord appeared to them there and said, "Peace be with you."[3]
- It was in this room that the disciples waited for the gift of the Holy Spirit at Pentecost.[4]
- Our last glimpse of Mary, the Mother of Jesus, was there, continuing in one accord with the disciples in prayer.[5]
- It was probably to this Upper Room that St. Peter came after his escape from prison in Jerusalem.[6]

Tradition has it that the present site of the 14th-century *cenaculum*[7] is probably the site where the Upper Room stood. It became known in the writings of St Cyril of Jerusalem (AD 348) as "The Upper Church".[8]

Our Lord's reaction to impending suffering was not one of bitterness or panic but of *calm preparation.* In those last hours he thought more of preparing and providing for others than he thought of himself. His provision for his disciples was to procure an Upper Room where he could be alone and quiet with them, and prepare himself and them for the ordeal that faced them. That room became sacred by its associations. "Having loved his own ... he loved them to the end."[9] He prepared them for their future service in the world by giving them a pattern to follow, setting them an example of prayer, and by celebrating with them the Passover Feast.

HE GAVE THEM A PATTERN FOR SERVICE

He had said of himself, "I am among you as the one who serves."[10] Now he took a towel, a badge of service. We often take a towel! As mothers we have a particular opportunity for service to our families and to each other. But for Jesus, who knew that he came from God and that he would return to God, to take a towel was an act of supreme humility.[11] He, the King of Glory, knelt down before each disciple to do this most menial task, to wash their feet. He knelt before Judas and washed his feet, though he knew he was about to betray him. This was a wonderful divine reaction to his enemy. He loved him even unto the end. "I have given you an example," he said, "that you should do as I have done to you."[12] Loving service is not so much what I do, as the way that I do it.

HE PREPARED THEM BY PRAYER IN THE UPPER ROOM

It has been said that our Lord won all his battles first on his knees in prayer. This was so before his temptations,[13] before his public ministry,[14] before his miracles of healing,[15] and in the Garden of Gethsemane.[16] Now, before his arrest and trial, we read, "Jesus ... lifted up his eyes to heaven and said, 'Father, the hour has come, glorify your son, that your son also may glorify you.'"[17] He poured out his heart in prayer. He had always maintained unbroken fellowship with his Father. He was to die as he had lived, committing himself and his disciples to his Father in prayer. We should pray rather than faint.[18]

HE PREPARED THEM AT THE PASSOVER FEAST[19]

This was the great Jewish festival to celebrate the deliverance of the children of Israel from the death which came to the firstborn of the Egyptians, who had not sacrificed a lamb without blemish.[20] St. John the Baptist had had a vision of this Last Supper when our Lord offered himself as the Pascal lamb, when he had said, "Behold! The Lamb of God who takes away the sin of the world."[21] In the words of the hymn, "There was no other good enough to pay the price of sin."[22]

Jesus took the ordinary bread and wine of the Passover Supper and lifted them up into an everlasting sacrament of his life and presence. In the Jewish Passover, he would have taken bread and said, "This is the bread of affliction your fathers did eat." Jesus now took the bread and said, "This is my body which is given for you."[23] In the Upper Room he left us this great sacrament of his redeeming life and love. There is nothing we can do for ourselves but what he has done for us and will continue to do. He communicates his life to us, his strength, his purity, his grace. He made this trysting or meeting place. Above the clamour and the dangers of Jerusalem was the haven of the Upper Room.

The Upper Room in our lives must dominate all the other rooms. Our church can be to us the haven of this Upper Room, or it can be the room in our house where we pray daily, a place the branch abides in the Vine.[24]

PRAYER

Blessed Lord, who for our sakes was content to bear sorrow and want and death, grant us such a measure of your Spirit that we may follow you in all self-denial and tenderness of soul. Help us by your great love to succour the afflicted, to share the burdens of the heavy laden and ever to see you in all that are poor and desolate, through Jesus Christ our Lord. Amen.[25]

Notes

[1]   The Upper Room (I) and The Upper Room (II) were talks given at Glandor Mothers' Union Quiet Day, at the Retreat House, Adelaide, April 10, 1968 (Holy Week). They draw on the last converse of Jesus Christ with his disciples before his crucifixion, both in St. John's Gospel and in the other three Gospels, though while the latter place this within the context of a Passover Meal, John does not. This combination of the two accounts, familiar to us from Maundy Thursday evening services today, reveals a rich spiritual legacy that Christ left his Church. Mother added to her talks a number of prayers. In this transcript we have kept just three and modernised their language.

[2]   This is only a possibility.

[3]   John 20:19, 26, Luke 24:36. It may have been the same venue, but this is not certain.

[4]   Acts 1:13. This is more likely as it is referred to here as "the" upper room.

[5]   Acts 1:14.

[6]   See note 2.

[7]   "Dining room, usually in an upper story; hence ... an upper room" (Lewis and Short, *A Latin Dictionary*, OUP).

[8]   *Catechetical Lecture* 16.4. Cyril is referring to the place where the Holy Spirit descended on the disciples at Pentecost.

[9]   John 13:1.

[10]   Luke 22:27.

[11]   John 13:3-4.

[12]   John 13:15.

[13]   Luke 3:21.

[14]   Mark 1:35.

[15]   cf. Luke 5:15-16.

Notes Continued

[16] Mark 14:36.

[17] John 17:1.

[18] cf. Luke 18:1.

[19] This is not given in John's Gospel, but in the other three Gospels.

[20] Exodus 12.

[21] John 1:29.

[22] From the hymn 'There is a green hill', by Cecil Frances Alexander (1848).

[23] Luke 22:19.

[24] John 15:4.

[25] A prayer from one of the proposed revisions of the *1662 Book of Common Prayer* put forward in the 1920s, later published in *The Grey Book* (1933); prayer modified.

The Upper Room (II)

THE LEGACY THAT OUR LORD GAVE US IN THE UPPER ROOM

Grant, we pray, O merciful Lord to your faithful people pardon and peace, that they may be cleansed from all their sins and serve you with a quiet mind, through Jesus Christ, our Lord.[1]

Jesus had no earthly possessions to leave, but what he left his disciples was something more precious than any material possessions. He gave them peace (Greek *eirene*). Peace heralded his coming.[2] He said to people, "Go in peace."[3] He used the Jewish salutation, "Peace be with you."[4] In John 14:27 we read, "My peace I leave with you ... not as the world gives, do I give to you. Let not your heart be troubled neither let it be afraid."

We can give each other a great deal in terms of sympathy and love but we cannot give each other peace of heart. What a time for Jesus to speak of peace when everything was trying to destroy it! He was in imminent danger of arrest and crucifixion. He was to go out of the Upper Room to the Garden of Gethsemane, then to the hall of judgement, then to Calvary.

PEACE WAS A QUALITY OF CHRIST'S CHARACTER

His personal peace was to be distinguished from the peace of outward circumstances. It came from the assurance of a perfect union, in thought, heart and will, with his Father in heaven. Christ's peace was like a white waterlily, tossed to and fro by the surface waves of the lake, but unshaken from its place because its roots are buried. He saw beyond the horizons of this world. "Who for the joy that was set before him endured the Cross, despising the shame."[5]

This oneness with his Father was shown throughout his life and in his prayer in the Upper Room: "That they all may be one, as you, Father, are in me, and I in you ... that the world may believe that you sent me."[6]

IS IT POSSIBLE FOR US TO HAVE PERFECT PEACE?

First, we must have peace with God, and then peace with each other. The collect we have used (above) prays that we may be granted pardon and peace – in that order. We need to know the peace of forgiveness and the restoration of a right relationship with God. We know what broken relationships can be in a family and how they ruin fellowship. Is there anything that comes between me and God? I must confess it. I must forsake before I can follow. In 1 John 1:9 we read, "If we confess our sins, he is faithful and just to forgive us our sins and to cleanse us from all unrighteousness;" it is "the blood of Jesus Christ ... [that] cleanses us from all sin" (1:7). We find the wonderful peace that our Lord gives us in forgiveness.

We must then be reconciled to each other. We must have forgiving hearts towards one another remembering Christ's words from the Cross, "Father, forgive them, for they know not what they do."[7] The people of Coventry have given us a fine example. Their cathedral was left in ruins after a German bombing raid[8] but, in the days that followed, three medieval nails that had fallen from the cathedral roof were formed into a cross, which was placed on the altar, and the words "Father forgive" inscribed in the chancel wall.

Jesus said, "If you bring your gift to the altar, and there remember that your brother has something against you, leave your gift there before the altar and ... first be reconciled to your brother, and then come and offer your gift."[9] "Teach me to do the thing that pleases you, O God," can be our prayer, guiding us to peace in our dealings with each other.

If we are maintaining a relationship which is not pleasing to God – get rid of it! Jesus said, "If your right hand causes you to sin, cut it off."[10] Peace is restored to us when we are reconciled to God and reconciled in our human relationships. We cannot reap the fruit of peace when we sow the seeds of war.

Our Lord never promised us immunity from evil. He left us his peace in the midst of evil. "The peace of God, which surpasses all understanding, will guard your hearts and minds,"[11] or garrison or fortify your heart against all invaders. At the heart of every cyclone there is a quiet place where a leaf will not stir, where a babe can sleep undisturbed. At the heart of every sorrow or bereavement, we should pray, "Into your hands I commit my Spirit."[12] Our Lord can give us this peace, which comes from faith and trust in him and from surrender to his will.

He said, "*Let* not your heart be troubled, neither let it be afraid." We can either let our hearts be troubled or let them be untroubled. That little permissive word is in our own wills; it is like the latch on the gate that leaves it shut against all intruders or wide open to all intruders. Peace is the gift of the Holy Spirit and the fruit of the Holy Spirit.[13] The Comforter or Strengthener brings us peace.

114

Lord Jesus, by your own peace of soul
Rooted and living in the eternal Father,
Serene in the hours of commotion and anguish,
Grant me your tranquillity.
Be my life hid in yours,
Let your fearless and imperturbable
Spirit come to dwell in mine.
Whom then, what then shall I fear?
You who guide us in the calm
Will not leave us in the storm.
So let me be still and inwardly worship
In private, in public, everywhere, always
And know that you are God,
My God, God with me.
Be the rock of my repose,
The moving pillar, before and behind
My pilgrimage.
Not as the world gives,
Giving your Peace.[14]

Notes

[1] *Book of Common Prayer, 1662*, 'Collect for the Twenty-First Sunday after Trinity', modernised.

[2] Luke 2:14.

[3] Mark 5:34, Luke 7:50.

[4] Luke 24:36, John 20:21, 26.

[5] Hebrews 12:2.

[6] John 17:21.

[7] Luke 23:34 (KJV).

[8] November 14, 1940.

[9] Matthew 5:23-24.

[10] Matthew 5:30.

[11] Philippians 4:7.

[12] Luke 23:46.

[13] Galatians 5:22.

[14] Origin unknown.

Lady Day[1]

A week ago on Sunday was Mothering Sunday. It is a day which children keep in loving remembrance of their mothers. By ancient custom in England, children give their mothers posies of primroses and violets on Mothering Sunday. Today on Lady Day we remember the greatest of all mothers – the mother of our Lord. We want to think of:

1) her strength;
2) her surrender;
3) her song.

MARY'S GREAT STRENGTH LAY IN THE FACT THAT SHE HAD "FOUND FAVOUR WITH GOD"[2]

St. Luke gives us most of our knowledge about her. It is thought that he, as a doctor, was *her* doctor, and so she had told him the intimate details of the pre-birth and birth of our Lord and of his childhood. He records the angel saying, "Do not be afraid, Mary, for you have found favour with God."[3] She had found what matters most in life – favour with God. She must have often prayed with the Psalmist, "Help me to do the thing that pleases you."[4] We can check all *we* do by this test: Are there things in my life which have not found favour with God? My occupations? What I do in my home? My pleasures?

In the last verse of St. Luke's second chapter we see how Mary's divine Son Jesus "increased in wisdom and stature and in favour with God". Her Son grew in the same direction as she was growing – towards God. In all her love and care of him, this is what mattered most to her – that he should find favour with God. "Train up a child in the way he should go: and when he is old, he will not depart from it."[5] Even if he departs for a while, he will come back to it. In early childhood, all the foundations are laid for life. On those early foundations is built the whole structure of life. All habits, both good and bad, are formed in childhood; habits of cleanliness and order, of truthfulness, of unselfishness, of prayer. Habits formed in childhood will not easily be broken. We read that Jesus used to go to the synagogue "as his custom was",[6] or as his habit was. He increased in favour with God. Mary put this first in her household. The blame for the delinquent behaviour of children does not lie so much with them as with their parents.

"Let it be to me according to your word."[7] The wonderful, unconditional surrender of our Lady! She had no idea where it would lead her. It led to hardship:

- Imagine what it meant for her to be the source of gossip amongst the neighbours!
- Imagine what it meant for her to take that tiring journey to Bethlehem just when her babe was to be born. To be shut out. To leave behind the things she had prepared for him at home.
- Think what it meant for her to become a refugee from her home country to Egypt for two years.

You would have expected her to *escape* suffering because she was so highly favoured, but no, even at the joyous moment of offering her infant son to God, the shadow of the Cross fell upon them both as Simeon predicted, "A sword will pierce through your own soul also."[8] We never read that she complained, but that she "kept all these things in her heart".[9] That was the safest place to keep them. No gossip.

MARY'S SOUL WAS REVEALED IN HER SONG

It burst forth from her spontaneously: "My soul magnifies the Lord."[10] Her soul was steeped in the Scriptures. She knew many of the psalms by heart, and her song revealed her knowledge of God.

What do *we* magnify most in life? Ourselves? – "I... I... I." Each other's faults? Our troubles? Mary magnified the Lord. People seeing her would see the Lord. As with a magnifying glass, she brought him close and made him clear to others. Do we make it easier for others to see the Lord or harder?

The secret of her strength is revealed in her song: "My spirit has rejoiced in God my Saviour."[11] In all joys and sorrows, he was the source of her strength. This was her hidden life of rejoicing in God her Saviour. We must return again and again to this hidden source of strength. Let us gain from her strength, her surrender and her song, in continually finding favour with God.

Notes

[1] The feast of the Annunciation of the Blessed Virgin Mary (March 25). This talk was given in 1969.

[2] Luke 1:30.

[3] *Ibid.*

Notes Continued

4 cf. "Teach me to do the thing that pleaseth thee, for thou art my God." (Psalm 143:10, 1662 BCP).

5 Proverbs 22:6.

6 Luke 4:16.

7 Luke 1:38.

8 Luke 2:35.

9 Luke 2:51.

10 Luke 1:46.

11 Luke 1:47.

The Love of Jesus[1]

We have seen Mary at the cradle. Now we see Mary at the Cross. The shadow of the Cross fell upon her. Those who have come to Bethlehem must inevitably follow on to the Cross. Joy and sorrow are so intertwined. She who was highly favoured had to come under the yoke of suffering. The sword pierced her own soul. She knew the deepest anguish of all – that of seeing her beloved suffering, and of being helpless to do anything to ease his agony. She would rather have been crucified herself than see it happen to him.

MARY WAS AT THE FOOT OF THE CROSS

That is the place where we must all come to see the fullness of the love of God and to experience his forgiveness. Mary came close enough to hear Jesus' words. She did not stand afar off. "Let me come closer, Lord Jesus."[2]

FORGIVENESS

She came close enough to hear his voice of forgiveness. She heard him say to those crucifying him, "Father, forgive them; for they know not what they do."[3] She also heard his words of forgiveness to the dying thief when he cried out, "Lord, remember me when you come into your kingdom," and Jesus' reply, "Today you will be with me in paradise."[4]

There is forgiveness for all *my* sins if I come close enough to the Cross. "Nothing in my hand I bring." There is nothing that I can do to take away my guilt – "simply to thy Cross I cling".[5] When Mary stood at the foot of the Cross, she came close enough to see a fresh revelation of Jesus' love for her.

JESUS' LOVE

In his agony, Jesus' thought was not of his own suffering but of hers. "Jesus ... saw his mother and the disciple whom he loved."[6] He saw their need as greater than his own. He saw Mary's need of care and protection. He saw her need of a home. He saw what the loss of a son meant to her – and he sees what *our* losses mean to us. He saw for Mary the emptiness of life and so, in his great love, he sought to fill that emptiness. His divine provision gave Mary and John to each other. "Woman, behold your son; son, behold your mother." And from that hour, John took her into his own home.[7] Peter, in all his misery and remorse,[8] must have gone to them – they must have given him refuge.

Jesus makes provision for us. Never can we escape his love. The nearer we draw to the Cross, the clearer we see his love and hear his words. He stoops down from the Cross in love to succour us – to provide for us. There is no experience that we can go through where he does not provide the strength. Even death. "Nothing in my hand I bring..." He can make even the very things that would be the stumbling blocks into stepping stones to bring us nearer to God. When we come close to the Cross, we receive forgiveness, the fullness of God's love and a new relationship with each other. "Mother, behold your son; son, behold your mother." Other people in need become our concern because God loves them and gave himself for them.[9]

Notes

[1] From the opening of this talk it could be a sequel to the previous one, though we cannot be certain.

[2] Perhaps an echo of the hymn, 'Let me come closer to Thee, Lord Jesus', by Joseph Leycester Lyne (19th century).

[3] Luke 23:34 (KJV).

[4] Luke 23:42-43.

[5] From the hymn 'Rock of ages', by Augustus Montague Toplady (1776).

[6] John 19:26.

[7] John 19:26-27.

[8] Matthew 26:75.

[9] Galatians 2:20.

Appendices

APPENDIX 1
Pocahontas and Gravesend[1]

When my husband was invited to give an address in Philadelphia, we were amused to see a notice that announced the Visiting Preacher would be "Dr Daunton" and he would be speaking on "Fear of Gravesend"!

St George's Church, Gravesend was built on the River Thames opposite Tilbury. It was a special landmark for pilots. Beneath the floor of the chancel was the burial place of Pocahontas, the first Red Indian convert to Christianity in America. Little did we know, when we moved to Gravesend, how much she would occupy our attention in the next few years!

When we arrived in Gravesend in 1948, St George's Church was proposed for demolition. This aroused much opposition. A letter by Sir Evelyn Wrench, opposing the scheme, was published in *The Times* newspaper. The Governor of Virginia rang the Rector to make his protest known. But my husband's response was, "I can't keep the church open on sentiment – help me!" This the Americans agreed to do, if half the money needed was raised in England. By gigantic effort, and the help of Miss Joan Apperley, the British half was raised,[2] and in 1951 we flew to America. Our tour was arranged by the English-Speaking Union.

We flew from London Airport to New York in 12 hours – now it takes six hours! The long night seemed lengthened by the time difference of five hours. Eventually we saw the sunrise. We landed at Idlewild Airport while most Americans were having breakfast. Our first impressions as we drove into New York, approaching across the river, were of the amazing skyline with its silhouette of skyscrapers, and of the vast number of pastel-coloured, streamlined taxis that filled the main roads. We spent a week in New York. The lights of Broadway (on day and night) dim all the lights of the cities of the world! We were impressed by the high-speed efficiency of life and the superb hospitality and generosity of the people. Also, the churches were so beautifully maintained. We spent a further week in a rectory in Richmond, Virginia where, apart from breakfast, only one meal was taken in the house.

Our main object in going to Virginia was to visit the part of the country most associated with Pocahontas. She is one of the most beloved figures in American history. Her father was the fierce, mighty Chief

Powhatan. Many claimed ancestry from Pocahontas – but what about Powhatan?! She did more to influence the fate of the Western Continent than any other woman in the world.

We were taken to see the actual foundations of the first English colony, built in 1607 by one hundred Englishmen who had braved the hazards of the sea in three small ships. This early colony was built on the banks of the James River, named by them in honour of our king. Looking out as we did over the wide, peaceful river, it was difficult to imagine the dangers it held for them. They lived in constant fear of death from the Red Indians and of famine and disease. Under these conditions began the settlement of Virginia. Every stroke of the axe and the fall of the trees meant the building of America's future. They faced terrible hardship, disease, famine and death.

Captain John Smith, one of the settlers, renowned for his bravery, led a group into enemy territory to trade for corn with the Indians. He was captured and dragged before Powhatan. His head was forced down on the stones. Suddenly Pocahontas, youngest and most loved daughter of Powhatan, sprang from the crowd and flung herself over John Smith's body, imploring her father not to kill him. Fixing him with her great imploring eyes she laid her head upon John Smith's. The club being wielded would kill her first. The old Chief relented, and a pipe of peace was lit.

Time and again, Pocahontas saved the settlers from starvation by bringing them food and warning them of attack. John Smith wrote to Queen Anne, "...she next under God was still the instrument to preserve this colony from death, famine and utter confusion."[3] Later, the Governor of the settlement kept Pocahontas as a willing hostage, to be returned to her father when certain Englishmen were returned from being his prisoners. During her stay at Jamestown, she lived with the family of a clergyman called Alexander Whitaker. He instructed her in the Christian faith. She was baptised and confirmed and attended the little church which we saw. During this time, she met a young widower, an Englishman called John Rolfe. In 1614 he married her and took her to visit his stately home in England, called Heacham Hall in Norfolk. On their arrival in London with their only son, Thomas, they were welcomed and entertained lavishly by the Bishop of London and she was presented at Court. Poor little thing, she yearned for her native land. Two years later, she sailed for Virginia from Gravesend but was taken ill and died on board. Her body was taken ashore and buried in St George's Church.

Following the successful fund-raising campaign, St George's became England's first ecumenical Chapel of Unity and a memorial to Pocahontas.

Notes

[1] The place and occasion of this talk are not recorded; possibly it was delivered in Australia.

[2] See the Introduction to this book, note 10. Presumably the figures given there include the money raised in America.

[3] Quoted verbatim from the letter John Smith wrote to Queen Anne in 1616. For the full text visit:

www.digitalhistory.uh.edu/active_learning/explorations/pocohontas/pocoho ntas_smith_letter.cfm

APPENDIX 2
Public Speaking on Devotional Matters[1]

Language is the communication of thought. Without it we should become isolated from each other, like islands. How often we say to one another, "*Tell* me what is in your mind." There is a great need for communication between the Church and the world. There is a similar need between nations, between employers and employees, between State and citizens, and between individuals.

The mind and thoughts of God have been communicated to us by his Son. In Hebrews 1:1-2 we read, "God, who at various times and in various ways spoke in time past to the fathers by the prophets, has in these last days spoken to us by his Son." And in John 1:1, 14: "In the beginning was the Word, and the Word was with God, and the Word was God … And the Word became flesh and dwelt among us, and we beheld his glory."

God bridged the gulf between himself and humans through language. We have to bridge the gap with language too. The right selection of words is important to communicate thought. It must be, in the *Prayer Book* term, language "understanded of the people".[2] John Wesley, feeling his mission was to the people of the English countryside, made it his practice to rehearse his address to the little country maid living in his household.

SPEAKING IS NOT JUST READING A PAPER

That lets us off too easily. Those are the speakers 'who speak in another's sleep'! Speakers must be prepared to use their whole personality to emphasise their words. The voice, above all, must not be monotonous. It must have the right tone, the right pitch and above all, clear diction.

PREPARATION FOR SPEAKING STARTS WITH THE PREPARATION OF THE SPEAKER

We often expect God to bless a slovenly preparation. Preparation in prayer beforehand is essential. We must pray both for ourselves and for the people to whom we shall be speaking. You may find it helpful to use the words of the hymn 'Breathe on me Breath of God'[3] or 'Come Holy Ghost, our souls inspire'.[4] Often I use this prayer: "Dear Lord, take my mind and think through it. Take my lips and speak through them. Take my heart and cleanse it and set it on fire with your love, and every life I touch, please kindle and bless."

CONSTRUCTION OF AN ADDRESS

First, select a theme or a subject. Read all you can on it. Use commentaries and devotional books, making notes. Then write a skeleton of what you want to get across to people. Develop it and then write it out fully. Go back to the skeleton notes for the delivery of the talk.

One of this century's greatest speakers has said, "First of all, be sure of your destination." Be sure of what you are driving at so that people don't say afterwards, "What on earth was he driving at?" The same speaker tells us that anyone delivering an address must begin, he must travel and he must arrive.

BEGIN

In his introduction the speaker must make vital contact with his listeners. He should say something startling in his first sentence. An audience can be lost or gained in the first sentence. According to your audience, make your contact with something familiar to them. It could be something topical.

Having procured their attention, tell them your subject or text, remembering that, though it is filling your own mind, it has not yet even been introduced to theirs.

TRAVEL

Take your audience with you – don't leave them behind! Have your material under *three headings* which are easily remembered. You must have pegs on which to hang your thoughts.

Travel towards a climax in your third point. Every address must have a climax. Any illustration or story needs to come in the third point. Don't continue or digress beyond it except to conclude. Beginnings and endings must never be too long or else people will grow bored. It is awful to hear a speaker saying, after talking for twenty minutes, "The subject I want to speak to you on tonight is…"!

ARRIVE

Bring your audience to their destination. Apply what you have been talking about to them personally. Leave them with the sense that this message was for them.

Addendum

In her course on speaking to the church women of Armidale Diocese in 1963 Mother made extra points. We record here what she said on the important matter of 'Visualisation':

There is an Arab proverb: "He is the best speaker who can turn the ear into an eye." Visual aids for teaching children have to be discarded for adults. In their place we must give them mental pictures and visualisation. What we *see* we don't easily forget. We make mental pictures far more often than we realise. For example, "A car rushed down the steep hill and crashed into the stationary truck at the bottom." We all visualised what happened here quite naturally. Peter Marshall[5] attended lectures at a theological college and listened to the professor say, "In speaking use sanctified imagination." This he developed in his own preaching and later said, "Pictorial preaching is the most effective because it is easier to get at the average mind by a picture rather than by an idea."

Our Lord presented deep spiritual truths in picture form through his parables. Paint Bible characters with living, warm colours. Bring them out of the dim distance of the past into the sharp clear focus of the present. For example, the "rich young ruler".[6] If we are going to make other people see, we must see him first ourselves.

Later in the course Mother turned visualisation to further good effect to enable her trainee speakers to have vital eye contact with their audience. This is what she said:

Don't have a lot of fussy notes that are very obvious and worry your audience. Have a folded sheet of paper that will not be noticeable in your open Bible as you hold it. It is a good idea to keep it in position with an elastic band so that it will not fall out.

At the top of your first page have your theme or text. Then your introduction. Then your first point[7] and a few notes of material. On the left-hand inside page have your second point. Add notes on material. On your right-hand inside page have your third point and notes on material. On your fourth, the back page, have the conclusion and application.

Now visualise the first page with its introduction and first point. Notice the underlinings and capital letters. Shut your eyes and see it. Visualise the second page with its second point. Visualise the third page, and the conclusion likewise. Look at each page in turn, shut your eyes

128

and visualise it. This means that, with visualising your material and your notes, you can look away at your audience and speak and not lose your place, and your eyes will fall on the right place in your notes when necessary.

This was Mother's own general approach, though she did not always start a new point on a new page.

Notes

1. A talk given to Lay-Readers on Speaking, in Adelaide, November 18, 1968.
2. Article 24 of the Articles of Religion (the 'Thirty-Nine Articles'), at the back of the *1662 Book of Common Prayer*.
3. By Edwin Hatch (1878).
4. By Bishop John Cosin, based on *Veni, Creator Spiritus* (1625).
5. Peter Marshall (1902-49), Scots American Presbyterian pastor and renowned preacher, husband of the celebrated Christian author Catherine Marshall.
6. Mark 10:17-21. In their accounts of this story, Matthew says the man was "young" (Matthew 19:22), and Luke says he was a "ruler" (Luke 18:18).
7. She had instructed them earlier to structure the sermon using three major points.

APPENDIX 3
The Ministry of Richard Daunton-Fear[1]

Associate of the London College of Divinity, 1931

Westcott House, Cambridge (Associate), Michaelmas 1931

B. en Th. (by equivalence), Faculté Libre de Théologie Protestante, Montpellier, 1934[2]

Queens' College Cambridge, M.A. (Natural Sciences) 1935

St. Chad's College Regina (Canada) L.Th. 1938, Honorary D.D. 1946

University of Bristol Research Student 1940, M.A. 1944[3]

Deacon January 3, priest December 27, 1932, Diocese of Southwark

Curate of St. John, Deptford, 1932-33

Rector of Woolland, Dorset, 1933-34

Rector of Aspenden, Hertfordshire, 1935-36

Rector of Denton with South Heighton and Tarring Neville, Sussex, 1936-38

Vicar of Lindfield, Sussex, 1938-40

Rector of Street, Somerset, 1940-44

Lecturer (Physics), University of Bristol, 1940-43

Vicar of Holy Trinity, Malvern, and Chaplain of Malvern Girls' College, 1944-48

Rector of Gravesend, 1948-53

Rural Dean of Gravesend 1949-53

Vicar of St. Mary, Shortlands, Kent, 1953

Prebendary of St. Mary-in-the-Castle, Exeter, from 1953

Vicar of St. Philip, Hove, 1953-59

Senior Chaplain to the Archbishop of Cape Town, 1959-60

Vicar of St. John, Tamworth, NSW, 1960-65

Archdeacon of Tamworth, 1960-65; Archdeacon Emeritus from 1965

Permission to Officiate in the Diocese of Chichester, 1965-66

Organising Chaplain of the Bishop's Home Mission Society, Diocese of Adelaide, 1966-70

Archdeacon of Gawler, South Australia, 1966-70

Permission to Officiate in the Diocese of Willochra, 1970-72 (living in Tumby Bay, SA)

Permission to Officiate in the Diocese of Winchester 1972-83 (living in St Helier, Jersey)

Hon. Chaplain of St. Matthew, Millbrook, Jersey, Diocese of Winchester, 1972-83 (retired 1973)

Permission to Officiate in the Diocese of Truro, 1983-87 (living in St. Austell, Cornwall)

Permission to Officiate in the Diocese of Chichester, 1987-91

Died Worthing, June 9, 1993

(Data taken from Crockford Clerical Directory, supplemented.)

Notes

[1] He was born Richard Daunton Fear on December 27, 1908. In Aspenden he changed his name by deed poll to Richard Daunton-Fear. In 1941 he changed it again to Richard Daunton Daunton-Fear, retaining this name for the rest of his life.

[2] For this Richard received lectures from the renowned theologian Karl Barth.

[3] For a thesis on Oliver Cromwell.